THE WORLD'S GREATEST LANDMARKS

Jerry Camarillo Dunn, Jr.

 Publications International, Ltd.

Writer Jerry Camarillo Dunn, Jr., is a longtime world traveler who has written books for *National Geographic* and the Smithsonian Institution, in addition to hundreds of travel stories for magazines and newspapers. He has appeared as a travel expert on CNN and teaches travel writing at the Santa Barbara Writers Conference. The Society of American Travel Writers has recognized his work with three Lowell Thomas awards, the "Oscars of travel writing." His newest book is *My Favorite Place on Earth* (National Geographic).

Fact-checker Victoria Garrett Jones has served as a researcher and writer for various historical, architectural, and travel-related publications including *National Geographic Atlas of World History* and *National Geographic Atlas of the 20th Century*. In addition, she has been part of research teams for *Builders of the Ancient World: Marvels of Engineering* and *Eyewitness to the 20th Century*. Jones has also written articles for *Traveler* and *World* magazines.

Pictured on the front cover, clockwise from top left: The Golden Pavilion (page 137); The Taj Mahal (page 126); Machu Picchu (page 43); The United States Capitol (page 17). Pictured on the back cover: Easter Island Statues (page 46).

Louis Weber, CEO

Publications International, Ltd.

7373 North Cicero Avenue

Lincolnwood, Illinois 60712

Permission is never granted for commercial purposes.

ISBN-13: 978-1-417-7710-0

ISBN-10: 1-4127-7710-0

Manufactured in China.

8 7 6 5 4 3 2 1

Library of Congress Control Number: 2008926777

When we build,
let us think that we build forever.

— *John Ruskin*

Contents

Introduction

Ever since a Greek poet named Antipater of Sidon compiled a roster of the Seven Wonders of the World in the second century B.C., people have made lists of awe-inspiring landmarks. Why? As a historical record? A guide for travelers? Or perhaps as a reminder that despite mankind's sorry catalog of wars and cruelty, we have also achieved the sublime—and left tangible proof for the ages?

The Seven Wonders of the Ancient World lay in the eastern Mediterranean, a part of the world where Antipater and his fellow Greeks could observe the legendary sights firsthand. Since then, the Colossus of Rhodes has tumbled; the Hanging Gardens of Babylon and other marvels have crumbled to dust and blown away like the torn pages of a calendar. Only one of the original wonders survives today, defying time, weather, and the overlay of succeeding civilizations: the pyramids at Giza.

Now it is time to add new landmarks to the list. But which works are worthy of

inclusion? Culling through the ancient, historic, and modern eras, this book nominates 57 landmarks for the roll of glory— from the ineffable white Taj Mahal to the inspirational Statue of Liberty to the

ancient Peruvian city of Machu Picchu, lost in clouds.

Whatever the builders' intentions— to create beauty, to assert power, to bid for a place in eternity, or simply to outdo what had been done before—all have left lasting marks on the planet. Some of the builders' purposes are clear, as in the case of the Roman Baths in Bath, England, but others remain as unknown and mysterious as the statues on Easter Island.

The builders were sometimes motivated by religion: to create a sacred space at Stonehenge; to awe believers at St. Peter's in Rome; to educate at Java's monumental stupa of Borobudur, whose three-mile path to the top leads pilgrims past thousands of carvings that illustrate Buddhist doctrines. Of course, some builders intended the glory only for themselves. Take the pharaoh Ramses II,

The Cathedral of Saint Basil the Blessed sits at the southern end of Moscow's Red Square next to the Kremlin. To many people around the world, this cathedral is seen as a symbol of Russia itself.

The Leaning Tower of Pisa, Italy, was plagued with problems from the start—it began to tilt while still under construction. Engineers have recently reduced the tower's angle, but they did not straighten it entirely. Local residents would not allow them to lose the lean altogether.

whose statues at Abu Simbel tower 65 feet tall—sitting down—and weigh as much as 1,200 tons. In Paris, Napoléon commissioned the Arc de Triomphe to honor his own victories on the battlefield. Other landmarks were constructed for military purposes, such as China's 4,000-mile-long defensive wall, or Syria's Krak des Chevaliers, a 12th-century Crusader castle whose fortifications were never breached by an enemy.

Finally, some landmarks fall into the category of "Why build it? Because we can!" Consider the Eiffel Tower, which took 150 to 300 workers two years to build from 18,000 metal parts and 2.5 million rivets—yet it was originally intended only as a temporary structure for a world's fair. Designer Gustave Eiffel himself noted that "France will be the only country in the world with a 300-meter flagpole."

Clearly, a roster of landmarks is also a catalog of superlatives. Take the Al-Haram Mosque in Makkah, which can hold 300,000 people at once. Or the cables supporting San Francisco's Golden Gate Bridge: Their bundled wires, with a total length of 80,000 miles, could wrap around the equator three times.

The very existence of the world's great landmarks inspires wonder. How did Egyptians living 4,500 years ago build the Great Pyramid at Giza, for example, somehow cutting, moving, and lifting 2.3 million blocks of limestone that weigh nearly three tons apiece?

Landmarks reveal much about the great cultures of the past, in the same way that books pass on the ideas and values of people who came before us. Newer landmarks reveal our own times—ingenious, high-tech structures such as the Guggenheim Museum in Bilbao, Spain; the Gateway Arch in St. Louis; and the Sydney Opera House in Australia.

New or old, the great landmarks send messages written in stone and sweat. What they say will endure for the ages.

The greatness of a landmark shows up as often in the details as in the structure itself. François Rude's scene of The Departure of the Volunteers in 1792 *(also called* The Marseillaise) *adorns the façade of the Arc de Triomphe.*

Empire State Building

The soaring symbol of New York City, the Empire State Building ranked as the world's tallest building for more than 40 years after it opened in 1931. Yes, size matters, but the skyscraper has other features even more appealing than its towering height. High on the list is the sheer pluck of its several thousand construction workers, who put in seven million total hours and set a record pace—the building was open for business only one year and 45 days after construction began.

Today most visitors—and there are more than 3.8 million per year—come for the panorama from observation decks on the 86th and 102nd floors. On a clear day they can see the whole layout of New York City, and the view from the 102nd floor extends 80 miles into four other states.

The building has had an interesting relationship with airplanes over the years. In the movie *King Kong* (1933), the giant ape stands on the summit of the building and swats at buzzing planes. The tower atop the building was initially planned as a mooring mast for dirigibles, a hazardous idea that was soon abandoned. In 1945 a B-25 bomber accidentally rammed into the building's 79th floor, gouging a 20-foot hole in the side, causing the edifice to shudder, and killing more than a dozen people (including the pilot).

A beloved feature of the New York City skyline, the Empire State Building shares the heights with such architectural wonders as the Chrysler Building (far right), a masterpiece of art deco design, which was the world's tallest building until the Empire State Building edged it out in 1931.

The framework of the Empire State Building contains 60,000 tons of steel. Technically, the structure reaches 1,454 feet, if you include the television mast.

Amazingly, the building's structural integrity wasn't compromised.

Equally remarkable are some Empire State Building statistics: The structure rises 1,250 feet and rests on more than 200 concrete-and-steel pilings. There are more than seven miles of elevator shafts, in which 73 elevators climb at speeds up to 1,400 feet per minute. Some ten million bricks wrap the exterior, whose 6,500 windows are washed continuously. About 20,000 people work in more than two million square feet of offices.

Lightning strikes the building about 500 times a year. Under certain conditions, so much static electricity builds up on the outdoor deck of the 86th-floor observatory that lovers get an extra tingle when they kiss here. It is a particularly romantic spot at night, with all the lights of Manhattan glowing below.

Guggenheim Museum

Among all the works of modern art on view at New York City's Guggenheim Museum, the great masterpiece is the building itself. Designed by the most famous and arguably the most innovative architect of the 20th century, Frank Lloyd Wright, the building was controversial from its opening day in 1959. A round building that bobs like a cork in a sea of square structures along Fifth Avenue, it announces its presence in no uncertain terms. The design is essentially an upside-down ziggurat, which is a Babylonian pyramidal temple whose successive stories rise in ever-diminishing size.

Observers pro and con have likened the upended spiral to a giant white shell, a washing machine, and an expandable plastic cup. But one thing is certain: Once you're inside, the museum is, without a doubt, user-friendly. Wright rebelled against the typical museum's layout, in which visitors pass through a succession of connected rooms only to retrace their steps to get out again. Instead, the architect decided to carry visitors by elevator to the top of the building and let

them stroll downward at an unhurried pace along a continuous spiral ramp whose walls are lined with paintings. The collection ranges from Impressionist art through nonobjective paintings and present-day works.

To achieve the museum's design, Wright created six sets of plans and 749 drawings during a 15-year period of both creativity and clashes with building authorities and public opinion. He told his clients—philanthropist Solomon R. Guggenheim and the millionaire's artistic advisor, Hilla Rebay—that he aimed to create "one extended, expansive, well-proportioned floor space from bottom to top . . . gloriously lit from above." At the top of Wright's more than one-quarter-mile-long spiraling ramp, 92 feet above the ground floor, there is a frosted glass dome that admits a cascade of light to flood the entire building. In this way, the architect fulfilled Rebay's directive: "I want a temple of spirit."

Opposite: *"I need a fighter, a lover of space, an agitator, a tester, and a wise man,"* said Hilla Rebay, who hired architect Frank Lloyd Wright to design the museum on behalf of copper magnate Solomon R. Guggenheim. Left: *"One of the greatest rooms erected in the 20th century,"* said modern architect Philip Johnson about Wright's spiraling levels of cream-colored concrete. The Who's Who of artists represented in the Guggenheim collection include Cézanne, Gauguin, Van Gogh, Picasso, Chagall, Kandinsky, Brancusi, and Mondrian.

Statue of Liberty

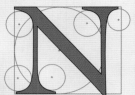

Nobler than an eagle, sweeter than apple pie, the Statue of Liberty reigns in the hearts of Americans as the true "first lady" of the United States. Since 1886 she has stood on an island in New York Harbor, holding aloft a torch—a welcoming beacon for immigrants, and the very symbol of freedom.

The statue was first proposed by French historian Édouard-René Lefebvre de Laboulaye to memorialize the friendship between the United States and France. Sculptor Frédéric-Auguste Bartholdi built the statue in Paris, using the woman who later became his wife as the model for the fig-

Left: *The formal name of the statue is "Liberty Enlightening the World." With its torch considered a lighting aid to ships, the statue was initially maintained and operated by the U.S. Lighthouse Board.* Opposite: *From 1892 to 1954, the Statue of Liberty welcomed more than 16 million immigrants into New York Harbor, among them movie mogul Samuel Goldwyn, comedian Bob Hope, and the von Trapp family singers of* The Sound of Music *fame.*

ure, his mother for the face. He began with a clay model about four feet tall, then made three successive enlargements. The final sculpture was created by using a full-scale plaster model and building wooden forms over its contours. Craftsmen then hammered the statue's copper skin over the forms. The skin is made up of 300 copper sheets, each not quite as thick as two pennies.

Meanwhile, engineer Gustave Eiffel (who would later become famous for his Eiffel Tower in Paris) took on the job of creating a framework capable of supporting the massive statue in the high winds of New York Harbor. His structure has a central pylon supporting a system of iron bars on which the copper shell hangs. This system is elastic enough to allow expansion and contraction during changes of temperature and flexible enough to withstand winds.

The statue's pieces were packed in 241 crates and shipped to New York for assembly. In accepting the gift, it was America's obligation to build a pedestal for it on Bedloe's (later renamed Liberty) Island. But Americans balked at the pedestal's cost, which would be nearly as much as that of the statue itself. The fund came up $100,000 short (and this is 1886 dollars). That amount was raised only after

newspaper publisher Joseph Pulitzer promised to print every donor's name in the *New York World,* regardless of how small the contribution. (In the process, the savvy Pulitzer considerably boosted the newspaper's circulation.)

American architect Richard Morris Hunt devised the neoclassical pedestal, mounting it upon an earlier star-shaped fortress on Bedloe's Island and designing it in concrete faced with granite. Inscribed on the base is the poem "The New Colossus," by Emma Lazarus. Many American schoolchildren have memorized the inspiring lines: "Give me your tired, your poor/Your huddled masses yearning to breathe free/The wretched refuse of your teeming shore/Send these,

the homeless, tempest-tost to me/I lift my lamp beside the golden door."

The pedestal shows off the great size of the statue, which had, in fact, been inspired by the Colossus of Rhodes, one of the Seven Wonders of the Ancient World. And what a colossal figure Bartholdi created. The statue stands 151 feet tall from its base to the tip of its torch and weighs 450,000 pounds (225 tons). Her waistline measures 35 feet around. Liberty's index

finger alone stretches eight feet long, and her fingernail is 13 by 10 inches.

In October 1886 President Grover Cleveland attended the dedication ceremony, where numerous speeches were delivered in a chilling rain. Then erupted a cacophony of cannons, foghorns, bands, whistles, and cheering that lasted for a quarter of an hour. About one million spectators had turned out for the festivities. (Before the event, New York police had rounded up

No part of the statue's skin rests directly on the parts below it, but instead is hung entirely on the iron skeleton. In this regard, the Statue of Liberty ranks as one of the first major curtain-wall constructions, a method applied to skyscrapers.

known pickpockets to prevent them from robbing the distracted spectators.)

The Statue of Liberty quickly became an American icon—as well as the queen of pop imagery and commercial exploitation, which began as early as the fund-raising campaign for the pedestal. The makers of Fletcher's Castoria offered a $25,000 donation, and all they asked in return was to display the brand name of their children's laxative for one year on the statue's massive base. Their offer was politely turned down. But since then Lady Liberty has served as a headpiece in wig advertisements, been made to disappear by a TV magician, and had her portrait done by Andy Warhol—not to mention appearing in the original *Planet of the Apes*.

In 1986 the Statue of Liberty observed her 100th birthday with a multi-million dollar facelift. The makeover included a new torch, its flame sheathed in brilliant gold leaf. The statue and its base still tower 305 feet from the ground to the tip of the torch, making it the largest metal statue ever created. Liberty reigns supreme over New York Harbor—and over the hearts of Americans, old and new.

Visitors to Liberty Island can climb 195 steps to the top of the statue's pedestal, or they can go all the way to the top—354 steps—to the observation deck in Lady Liberty's crown. The deck offers 25 windows, some of which allow a stunning view of New York City. This view is a highly coveted one, and lines can be long, with waits of up to three hours.

THE
United States Capitol

Washington D.C.

Perhaps the most prominent landmark in a city that fairly bursts with them, the United States Capitol overlooks Washington, D.C., from a lofty knoll. Its elevated site (now titled Capitol Hill but once humbly known as Jenkins Hill) was chosen in 1791 by the city's visionary designer, French engineer Pierre L'Enfant. He described the hill as "a pedestal waiting for a monument."

After holding a competition among hopeful designers of an appropriate monu-ment, President George Washington, Secretary of State Thomas Jefferson, and the commissioners of the recently estab-lished District of Columbia chose an unlikely winner whose proposal had arrived months after the deadline—a physician and amateur architect named Dr. William Thornton. Thornton's plan was modeled on the Pantheon in Rome, with a dome set atop a central cube. This was flanked by north and south wings to house the Senate and the House of Representatives.

Construction began in 1793 after a dedication ceremony at which George Washington, wearing full Masonic garb, laid the cornerstone. By 1800 both houses of Congress were able to move into the north wing, and shortly after that a new architect, Benjamin Henry Latrobe, com-pleted the south wing for the House of Representatives. His attention to detail shows in such elements as column capitals that are carved with emblems of the young nation's agricultural wealth: tobacco leaves and corncobs.

During the War of 1812, a setback occurred as British troops set fire to the Capitol in 1814. Rebuilt in only five years, the building later underwent various modifications. In the 1850s the

Left: *The artistic influences of ancient Greece and Rome show in the classical design of the U.S. Capitol, through its ornate Corinthian columns and sculp-tured pediments, its symmetry and grandeur. Opposite: Aglow by night, the dome of the U.S. Capitol appears almost weightless, even though it's made of cast iron. The Capitol grounds were laid out in the late 1800s by Frederick Law Olmstead, who also designed New York's Central Park.*

wings were rebuilt with chambers large enough to hold legislators from new U.S. states. The added width of the building was offset in 1863 by a new rotunda that soars 180 feet high. Its dome is made of cast iron and is topped with a statue of "Freedom," a goddess of democracy adorned with a feathered helmet.

The dome towers above the focal point of the Capitol, the Rotunda. Here, according to L'Enfant's plan, the city's north-south and east-west axes crisscross at the center of the room. On the canopy of the dome overhead, Italian artist Constantino Brumidi—who had fled to America to escape political persecution in Italy—painted a fresco titled *The Apotheosis of George Washington*. He also executed part of a frieze that depicts American history beginning with Columbus's landing in the New World.

Brumidi painted a corridor in the Senate wing with extravagant images of animals, plants, and American faces, set amidst Roman-style decorations. All this exuberance was a bit too much for Mark Twain, who termed the work the "delirium tremens of art."

The Capitol's monumental scale conveys the majesty of America's representative system of government—and, ultimately, the power of her citizens to chart the course of the nation's life.

At the Capitol's main entrance, bronze doors weighing 20,000 pounds illustrate Columbus's explorations. Throughout the building, paintings and statues portray American heroes and politicians. A bust of Abraham Lincoln—sculpted by Gutzon Borglum, who created Mount Rushmore— shows the president without a left ear, the sculptor's way of calling attention to the president's life having been tragically cut short.

Today the Capitol is crowded with modern legislators who wield immense power and set national policy. When they are in session, a lantern above the dome is lit—perhaps to inspire illumination among the lawmakers.

An ornate canopy fills the interior of the immense dome, which soars 180 feet high. Congress authorized this dome to replace a smaller one in 1855, and construction of the dome continued during the Civil War. Continuing to build, declared Abraham Lincoln, provided a "sign that we intend the Union shall go on."

The White House

The home of U.S. presidents for more than two centuries, the White House—despite being a neoclassical mansion—still reflects the American philosophy that a president is revered but not royal, of the people but not above them. Rooms and reception areas are built to a human scale (although Thomas Jefferson once wryly commented that the White House was "big enough for two emperors, one Pope, and the grand lama").

Designed by Irish immigrant Thomas Hoban after manor houses in Dublin, the White House has been altered by succeeding presidents to suit their tastes and times. Thomas Jefferson introduced the water closet (we call it a bathroom today); James A. Garfield, an elevator; Benjamin Harrison, electric lights; and Franklin D. Roosevelt, a pool. In the 1960s Jacqueline Kennedy oversaw a historically accurate redecoration. Later George Bush put in a horseshoe-throwing pit, and Bill Clinton added a jogging track.

The White House stands among 18 acres of lawns and gardens. Its extensive security devices are all but invisible, so it appears to be what it has always been—a stately home for America's head of state.

Cape Hatteras Lighthouse

North Carolina

One of America's most famous lighthouses, this is a shining beacon for ships venturing through the "Graveyard of the Atlantic," the treacherous seas and shoals near Cape Hatteras, North Carolina, that have claimed some 2,200 vessels.

Replacing an earlier, feeble beacon in 1870, the lighthouse stands on a low, sandy point subjected to perpetual wind, warning ships away from the barrier islands that make up the 130-mile-long Outer Banks region where Cape Hatteras lies. It has remained steadfast through 40 hurricanes and regularly faces ferocious storms. The tumultuous weather is brewed up just offshore where two opposing currents collide: the icy seas of the Labrador Current and the warm Gulf Stream.

The black-and-white stripes that spiral up the lighthouse make it immediately recognizable and serve as a daytime identification aid for boat traffic. By night, an automated beam flashes every seven-and-a-half seconds, a distinctive rate that helps ships to distinguish it from other nearby lighthouses. Two 1,000-watt bulbs send out these beams, each 800,000 candlepower, which can be seen 20 miles away. Remarkably, the bulbs are powered by ordinary house current. If one burns out, a spare bulb and reflector automatically rotate into place.

Cape Hatteras ranks as the nation's tallest lighthouse—193 feet, 2 inches. To ascend to the gallery level, visitors climb a steep, winding staircase. From up there they can sense the sheer mass of the structure below, which consists of 1.25 million bricks and weighs 9.4 million pounds. The beach on which the lighthouse stands has been a victim of erosion. Although the light once stood more than 1,500 feet from the breakers, by 1999 erosion had brought it nearly to the water's edge. In that year the federal government teamed with the North Carolina state government to move the lighthouse farther away from the ocean, protecting it for years to come.

Left: *In 1999, to protect the lighthouse from a steadily eroding beachfront, it was lifted, moved 2,900 feet, and set down on a new foundation—a remarkable feat of engineering.* Opposite: *Inside the lighthouse, a spiral staircase winds upward for some seven revolutions and 269 steps. Visitors climb up to the gallery, where they enjoy a spectacular view out to sea.*

Gateway Arch

Missouri

Whether it reflects the bright colors of sunset or fades into gray morning fog, the Gateway Arch in St. Louis, Missouri, makes an unforgettable sight. Measuring 630 feet from the ground to its highest point, the arch stands more than twice as tall as the Statue of Liberty. It soars above the bank of the Mississippi River like a stainless-steel rainbow.

Opened to the public in 1967 at a cost of $13 million, the "gateway" symbolizes St. Louis's role in America's westward expansion. Lewis and Clark's expedition left the city's environs in 1804 with a mandate from President Thomas Jefferson to discover what the nation bought for the less than three cents an acre it had spent on the Louisiana Purchase, that vast expanse of the continent stretching westward from the Mississippi River. The "Corps of Discovery" gathered scientific knowledge of the West's animals and plants, laid foundations for

Opposite: Dangers defeated: The arch can withstand high winds, moving no more than 18 inches at the top during a 150-mph gale. Lightning rods are mounted on top and grounded into the bedrock, protecting the interior from the electrical discharge of hundreds of bolts each year. Right: The legs of the arch, built simultaneously, were freestanding during construction until they met at the top. A stabilizing truss was added at 530 feet to hold them steady until the structure was complete.

future trade with the native cultures, and affirmed the claim the United States made over the Pacific Northwest. These are the sorts of things visitors can learn at the Museum of Westward Expansion, located beneath the arch.

The arch itself, designed by architect Eero Saarinen, is technically an inverted catenary curve (the type formed by a chain hanging between two pegs). Each leg has the shape of an equilateral triangle whose sides measure 54 feet at ground level, nar-

rowing to 17 feet at the top. To support the arch, reinforced concrete foundations sink 60 feet into the ground, half in bedrock.

A tram inside each leg carries visitors on a four-minute ride to the top of the arch. The trams, which combine the principles of the elevator and the Ferris wheel, were designed in just two weeks by a man with no college degree, Dick Bowser.

Atop the arch visitors gaze out through windows at the gently flowing Mississippi River and the city below. On a clear day they can see 30 miles—not nearly as far as Lewis and Clark's vision, but a good start.

Mount Rushmore

South Dakota

"There is not a monument in this country as big as a snuff box," complained Gutzon Borglum, a prolific American sculptor of the early 20th century who had studied in Paris with the great French artist Auguste Rodin. Then he was offered a project to match his visions. South Dakota's state historian approached him about carving an entire mountain. The official wanted a monument big enough to put his overlooked state on the map—and, not incidentally, to lure tourists.

The colossal result was Mount Rushmore National Memorial—four presidents' faces carved into a granite peak in the Black Hills. Borglum planned the monument "in commemoration of the foundation, preservation, and continental expansion of the United States." As his subjects, he chose four leaders who had guided

America from colonial days into the 20th century: George Washington (the first U.S. president), Thomas Jefferson (the author of

the Declaration of Independence and sponsor of westward expansion), Theodore Roosevelt (a supporter of the Panama Canal and early conservationist), and Abraham Lincoln (the leader who held the Union together and ended slavery).

Right: *Rough shaping of the colossal portraits was done with dynamite, which could carve away enormous amounts of the solid rock. Then chisels and air-driven hammers removed any remaining roughness, giving each face a smooth complexion.* Opposite: *Sculptor Gutzon Borglum intended that Mount Rushmore be "the formal rendering of the philosophy of our government into granite on a mountain peak." Mount Rushmore rises in the 1.2-million-acre Black Hills National Forest, a realm of crags softened by evergreen trees.*

The magnitude of the sculpture flabbergasts viewers. Washington's head is as tall as a six-story building. His nose alone is 20 feet long; his mouth, 18 feet wide. At this scale, Washington's full figure would stand 465 feet tall.

To shape the world's largest mountain sculpture, Borglum worked from 1927 to 1941. Six-and-a-half years were spent in actual carving, the rest were given to preparation and waiting for funds during the lean Depression years.

More than 80 percent of the work was done with a seemingly preposterous tool: dynamite. Only by blasting could he quickly and inexpensively remove the enormous amount of hard rock that was necessary. His crew grew so skilled that they could blast to within a few inches of the finished surface. As work progressed, Borglum made any needed changes to the original design—most notably, moving Jefferson's head from Washington's right side to his left, as there wasn't enough stable rock for the portrait as it was originally laid out.

After dynamiting, the workers bored a network of closely spaced holes, each reaching almost the depth of the finished surface. Then they used chisels to remove the surplus rock, and finally they

"The noble countenances emerge from Rushmore as though the spirit of the mountain heard a human plan and itself became a human countenance," said architect Frank Lloyd Wright—thus affirming that such a realistic monument can be pronounced a successful work of art in contemporary eyes.

George Washington's was the first head completed and was officially dedicated in 1930. It was during this dedication ceremony that Mount Rushmore was officially called "a shrine to democracy," a description that has endured through the years.

employed pneumatic hammers to smooth the "skin" of each face.

Both nature and art contrive to bring the presidential portraits to life. As the morning and afternoon sun play across their features, the faces appear mobile and relaxed. And in carving the eyes, Borglum employed a sculptor's trick. Within the pupils are projecting pieces of granite that, viewed from a distance, make the eyes sparkle with life.

The nearly 400 unemployed miners, ranchers, and loggers who did the dusty, bone-wearying work of blasting and carving had originally taken the job just to get a paycheck, but they came to feel a dedication nearly matching that of Borglum himself. "I put the curl in Lincoln's beard, the part in Teddy's hair, and the twinkle in Washington's eye," said driller Norman "Happy" Anderson. "It still gives me a thrill to look at it."

A Mount Rushmore carver named Red Anderson observed: "The longer we were there, the more we began to sense that we were building a truly great thing, and after a while all of us old hands became truly dedicated to it." The colossal sculpture fulfills Gutzon Borglum's vision: "A nation's memorial should, like Washington, Jefferson, Lincoln, and Roosevelt, have a serenity, a nobility, a power that reflects the gods...they have become."

Many visitors wonder how the mountain got its name, and the answer reflects the colorful early West. In 1885 a New York attorney named Charles E. Rushmore visited the Black Hills. He introduced himself to a local prospector and asked the name of the nearby 5,725-foot-high peak. In fact, the mountain had no name, but the prospector jokingly answered, "Mount Rushmore." The name stuck.

According to geologists, the hard, ancient granite of Mount Rushmore's carved faces will wear down at a rate of just one inch in every 10,000 years. Gutzon Borglum said that he breathed "a prayer that these records will endure until the wind and the rain alone shall wear them away."

Mesa Verde

Haunting, lovely, and enigmatic, these cliff dwellings perch on sheer stone walls in southwestern Colorado. They were built around A.D. 1200 by the ancestors of many of the nations currently in the area for reasons unknown to anyone now living. Novelist Willa Cather, after visiting the dwellings in 1916, wrote: "Such silence and stillness and repose—immortal repose. That village sat looking down into the canyon with the calmness of eternity."

Mesa Verde in Spanish means "green table," referring to the thickly wooded plateau occupied by the Ancestral Pueblo people. Around A.D. 500 these people first settled on top of the mesa in pithouses dug into the ground. To survive, they hunted mule deer and rabbits, grew corn, and raised turkeys. After about five centuries they started constructing villages of upright poles and adobe. Then around 1200 they moved down into the canyons, where, in alcoves created by seeping water, they built the cliff "palaces" that have brought fame to this place of red rock and endless sky.

The largest cliff dwelling of the Ancestral Puebloans to survive anywhere, Cliff Palace contains 217 rooms situated below an overhanging brow of rock. It sheltered perhaps 250 people and has 23 kivas, round underground chambers where men got together to weave and where ceremonies were held. (Since each family had a kiva, the number reveals how many different family groups or clans occupied Cliff Palace.)

The Ancestral Puebloans may have built their cliff dwellings for purposes of defense. Even today getting to Balcony House, for example, is tricky and involves climbing dizzying ladders and staircases and creeping through a narrow, 12-foot-long passage. To reach the three-story dwellings of Spruce Tree House means a steep hike of 100 feet down the mountain trail.

One of the great questions about Mesa Verde is why the Ancestral Pueblo people deserted their cliff dwellings within a hundred years of building them. Soil depletion? Drought? The disappearance of animals and firewood?

One more enigma in a place full of mystery.

Below: *A place of silence and mystery, Mesa Verde has been deserted since the 13th century. The Ancestral Puebloans were the first, last, and only inhabitants of the cliff dwellings. Opposite: In 1906 Mesa Verde was declared a national park, unique in protecting works of people, not nature. It had been looted regularly since the cliff dwellings were first entered by a U.S. government photographer in 1874.*

Hearst Castle

What can it be, that sparkle in the sunlight atop a hill on the central California coast? A fairytale palace? No, it is Hearst Castle, the beyond-belief estate of powerful publishing mogul William Randolph Hearst, once the head of the nation's largest newspaper chain and the reputed model for the ego-driven main character in *Citizen Kane,* the classic 1941 film by Orson Welles.

Hearst's 127-acre estate, designed by architect Julia Morgan, gives the impression that a bit of Europe has magically wafted to the Wild West. Starting work in 1919, Hearst and Morgan conjured up a Mediterranean hill town. Its buildings are arranged around a village plaza, with the role of cathedral played by the towering main house, La Casa Grande.

Hearst named the estate La Cuesta Encantada, "The Enchanted Hill." The main house and three guest houses—designed in Spanish Renaissance style, with a total of 165 rooms—are crammed with Hearst's collection of artwork, much of it from European castles and churches: choir stalls, French Gothic tapestries, carved Spanish ceilings.

Famous houseguests, who included glamorous movie stars such as Clark Gable and Jean Harlow, often visited from Los Angeles. As limousines carried them up the hill, they were surprised to see roaming lions, elephants, and other exotic animals—part of Hearst's private menagerie.

Free to enjoy every amenity, guests played tennis

More than a hundred feet long, the Neptune Pool shimmers beside an impressive Greco-Roman temple façade. It's no wonder that Hollywood stars enjoyed frolicking in the pool as guests of William Randolph Hearst.

or frolicked in the indoor Roman Pool, which is sheathed in blue glass and gold leaf. Winston Churchill, tour guides suggest, may once have floated here in an inner tube, never giving up his cigar.

In order to preserve the fond illusion that all this was simply a California ranch meant for camping out—that's how the estate began—Hearst had the dining room tables set not only with gleaming silver and porcelain, but also with bottles of ordinary ketchup. Quirky, over-the-top extravagant, but never to be forgotten—that's Hearst Castle.

The fabled estate's 127-acre grounds are resplendent with ancient statuary, tiled fountains, and gardens, all set around La Casa Grande and three guesthouses. Among other amenities, Hearst's domain boasted its own private movie theater, a library of more than 4,000 volumes, and a zoo of exotic animals.

Golden Gate Bridge

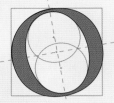 One of the most remarkable, yet least known, sights in San Francisco is the Golden Gate Bridge—that is, as seen from *below*. The curious who make their way to the footings at either end of the bridge get a rare look *up* at the vaulting arch as it soars across a mile-wide opening in the Pacific coastline. Depending on the weather, the lofty art deco towers may gleam in the California sunshine or seem to vanish overhead into shape-shifting fog.

The twin towers stand 746 feet high (comparable to a 62-story building) and together would tip the scales at more than 175 million pounds. As in all suspension bridges, the towers support cables from which the roadway is hung. Each cable weighs about 11,000 tons and encloses 27,572 wires. The total length of 80,000 miles of wire could wrap around the equator more than three times.

Workers have consistently been touching up the bridge's paint since it opened in 1937. The first coat required 10,000 gallons of vermilion paint. The bridge's vivid hue is officially named International Orange.

Still, painting the bridge was the least of chief engineer Joseph Strauss's worries. He had to meet the serious challenges posed by nature: strong winds, tidal surges moving through the Golden Gate as fast as 60 miles per hour, fog and rain, even earthquakes. He designed the center span to handle 27.7 feet of sway during a high wind or temblor. He managed to construct the south tower, which lies nearly a quarter-mile offshore, on a foundation that extends 110 feet below water level.

The Golden Gate Bridge ranks as one of the world's great works of engineering, yet it also soars to the level of art. Standing against a field of blue water and green headlands, the reddish-orange bridge appears in the landscape as a brilliant piece of sculpture.

Below: *A world-class feat of engineering or a transcendent work of art? Surely the Golden Gate bridge is both. The art deco bridge changes appearance throughout the day, especially when the fog rolls in.* Opposite: *Linking San Francisco to Marin County, the bridge stretches 8,981 feet, including approaches. The main span, at 4,200 feet, ranked as the longest in the world until 1964, when New York's Verrazano Narrows Bridge snatched the record. Today, the longest is Japan's Akashi Kaikyo Bridge, with a main span of 6,532 feet.*

CN Tower

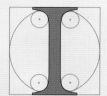

In Toronto, Canada's largest city, the CN Tower rises like an exclamation point. This single structure holds a number of superlatives, boasting the:

World's tallest building and free-standing structure!

Ontario

World's longest metal staircase! World's highest wine cellar! (It is located in a restaurant whose floor rotates once every 72 minutes to give diners a view of the city below.)

The tower stands 1,815 feet, 5 inches high, or the equivalent of 12 Statues of Liberty stacked on top of each other. (And while we're making comparisons, it weighs 130,000 tons, equal to 23,214 large elephants.)

Opened in 1976, the tower was developed by Canadian National, a Canadian railroad corporation, as a way to show off to the world that Canada had the industrial strength to construct such an engineering marvel. It has made Canadians proud ever since.

The tower also serves a practical purpose. After a 1960s building boom in Toronto, broadcasters found that their transmission towers weren't tall enough to send signals above the new skyscrapers, and the city's television and radio reception declined. The CN Tower, with its microwave receptors and antennas, cleared up the problem.

From the base of the tower, visitors are whisked aloft on six high-speed elevators with gasp-inducing glass fronts, traveling at 15 miles per hour and taking just 58 seconds to reach the Look Out level at 1,136 feet. Just one level below this, a glass floor puts Toronto literally at your feet; you're looking 1,122 feet straight down! (Relax, the glass is plenty strong. Comparison: The floor could support 14 large hippos.)

A separate elevator makes the final ascent of another 33 stories to the Sky Pod. From here, at 1,465 feet, you can enjoy a view of up to more than 100 miles in every direction—Toronto, Lake Ontario, and even Niagara Falls on a clear day. At the top of the tower, observers can actually look down on airplanes approaching the city airport.

The United Arab Emirates' Burj Dubai is slated to break the record for tallest building. As of this writing, the tower stands at 2,063 feet, and still rising.

Left: *At the 1,122-foot level, an outdoor observation area lets visitors feel the breeze. In stronger winds, the tower is designed to sway: During a 120-mph gale, the antennas can deflect 6 feet, 8 inches. Opposite: If you drank three cans of soda each day, it would take you more than four years to collect enough cans to stack as high as the CN Tower. At 1,815 feet, 5 inches high, the tower pierces low clouds.*

Pyramids of the Sun and Moon
AT TEOTIHUACÁN

Mexico

Towering and mysterious, the Pyramids of the Sun and Moon rise above silent Teotihuacán, an empty city that once bustled with as many as 200,000 people and stood at the center of Mexico's pre-Hispanic empire. Erected by a virtually unknown culture in the first century B.C., the city sprawled over an area larger than imperial Rome. But by A.D. 750 it had been abruptly abandoned, perhaps because of disaster or drought. Five hundred years later the Aztecs came upon Teotihuacán—with its pyramids, temples, apartments,

and ball courts—and adopted it as a center of pilgrimage.

At roughly 210 feet high, the Pyramid of the Sun ranks as one the largest pyramids in the world. (It is about half as tall as the Great Pyramid in Egypt.) The builders raised the Pyramid of the Sun around A.D. 100, somehow transporting and erecting three million tons of stone, brick, and rubble without benefit of the wheel, beasts of burden, or metal tools.

In 1971 archaeologists found a previously unknown entryway some 320 feet long that leads to a cave directly beneath the apex of the pyramid. At one time the cave held a natural spring, and there are still piles of charcoal in the chamber—perhaps indicating ceremonies involving water and fire. No one knows, although scientists enjoy speculating.

After climbing 248 steps to the top of the pyramid, you can survey the temple-lined Avenue of the Dead, a roadway about two-and-a-half miles long that ends with the Pyramid of the Moon rising to the north. Finished before A.D. 300, it appears to be as tall as the Pyramid of the Sun. In actuality, however, it is only 150 feet tall, built on higher ground. Twelve platforms once stood on the adjacent plaza, where religious dancing may have been performed. Again, no one knows. The mystery endures.

Left: *The pyramids stand along the Avenue of the Dead, a two-and-a-half-mile-long road named by the Aztecs, who believed it to be the burial place of a race of giant people who had evolved into deities. (Teotihuacán translates as "The Place Where Men Become Gods.")*
Opposite: *During its heyday around A.D. 600, more than 200,000 people lived in the ancient city. Archaeologists have mapped 2,000 apartments and catalogued more than a million artifacts, including pottery and stone tools.*

Chichén Itzá

Mexico

At Chichén Itzá travelers find the riddles of the Mayan calendar revealed in a "temple of time" and come face to face with the enigma of human sacrifice. Located on Mexico's Yucatán Peninsula, this is the region's most thoroughly restored Mayan site. Established in the fifth century, it declined after the Classic Maya period, then exploded with new energy as the militaristic Toltecs arrived, bringing new gods and fusing their culture with that of the Maya.

The dominant ruin, *El Castillo* (The Castle), incorporates Mayan astronomical knowledge into a subtly coded architecture. The pyramid rises in nine receding levels to a temple on top. Each face is divided in two by a monumental staircase, creating 18 terraces that symbolize the 18 months of the Mayan year. All four stairways have 91 steps; coupled with the top platform, the steps total 365, the days in the Mayan calendar. But the most remarkable display of

celestial awareness occurs only at the spring and autumn equinoxes. At sunset a shadow appears to ripple along the north staircase, forming a snakelike "body" that links the carved serpents' heads at the bottom to their tails at the top.

At the end of a stone road lies the Sacred Cenote, a natural well more than 100 feet across and some 115 feet at its deepest. Judging by the jewelry and the bones of adults and children found at the bottom by modern-day archaeologists, all sorts of offerings were thrown into the water to satisfy the gods.

Chichén Itzá also boasts Mexico's largest ancient ball court, with stone hoops that served as targets. Carvings show not only the game in progress but also a player holding up the head of the losing team's captain. Clearly, the mysterious game was played for keeps.

Nowadays, visitors to the ball court divert themselves by testing its amazing acoustics: A whisper can be heard 450 feet away. But there are no whispers from the past to explain the riddles that still surround Chichén Itzá.

Opposite: El Castillo is also known as the Pyramid of Kukulkán—the Mayan name for the feathered serpent god, Quetzalcóatl. Deep inside lies an earlier pyramid, which holds a throne in the shape of a red jaguar with jade eyes and flint fangs. Below left: A union of Toltec and Maya cultures developed Chichén Itzá from a village into a regional center, with various temples and the largest ball court in Mesoamerica. The settlement was named after a sacred well. Below right: The reclining figure of Chac-Mool was a pedestal for human sacrifice, holding a bowl where a human heart was placed, still beating after being ripped out of the victim's chest. The Toltecs considered sacrificial death a great honor.

Christ the Redeemer Statue

Brazil

With arms spread wide—as if to embrace the whole city of Rio de Janeiro sprawling below in spectacular disorder— the *Cristo Redentor* statue can be seen from all over town.

For a pedestal, the statue has the 2,310-foot mountain called Corcovado. The Christ figure on top rises another 100 feet, its arms extending nearly 92 feet from fingertip to fingertip, with a weight of some 700 tons. French sculptor Paul Landowski and his team of artisans erected the impressive statue to commemorate the hundredth anniversary of Brazil's 1822 independence from Portugal. Due to budget constraints, however, the centennial artwork was finished nearly a decade later in 1931, and then only with help from the Vatican. Sleekly contemporary in appearance, the statue was fashioned of soapstone and concrete.

The *Cristo Redentor* figure vies with Sugarloaf Mountain as the emblem

of the city of the *cariocas*. And its site offers a view over Rio that is even more spectacular than Sugarloaf's, taking in the famous beaches at Copacabana and Ipanema, tree-lined residential neighborhoods, the bay, and a blue lagoon called *Rodrigo de Freitas*. Corcovado itself is enveloped within a tropical reserve where

waterfalls tumble and butterflies flit through thick forests.

Local residents like to go up to see the statue by riding on a 2.3-mile cog railway whose tracks for cogwheel steam engines were laid up the mountainside in 1885. During the 20-minute ride, the train passes through leafy green tunnels of trees and provides views of Brazil's city of pleasure and poverty, carnival and beaches, far below.

In the evening, powerful spotlights illuminate the statue of Christ, making it glow and appear almost to levitate above the darkened peak. By day or night, no matter where you may go in the city of Rio, the statue has the presence of an icon.

Opposite: *After riding up the mountain by auto or cogwheel railway, visitors must climb more than 200 steps to the statue's base. The view is spectacular: Christ's right arm points to famous Ipanema Beach, the left arm toward the world's largest soccer stadium (Maracaña), Rio's international airport, and a mountain range.* Left: *Floodlights lend the towering statue a heavenly radiance. The name of the mountain upon which the figure rises, Corcovado, means "hunchback," a reference to its shape.*

Machu Picchu

Peru

A lost city floating in a kingdom of clouds. A stone Shangri-la set high in the Andes mountains of Peru. A mysterious settlement that the Incas built, occupied, and deserted, all in less than a century. This is Machu Picchu.

For hundreds of years the city was hidden in the jungle. Then, in 1911, a Yale professor named Hiram Bingham led a university expedition to the Peruvian Andes. On a valley floor along the Urubamba River, he met a farmer who guided him up to the ruins of the hidden city—the only Incan site that hadn't been looted or destroyed during the previous four centuries.

Looking at the city's finely cut stone buildings, Bingham thought he had discovered Vilcabamba, the legendary last refuge of the Incas. Eventually, however, archaeological evidence piled up to the contrary. Machu Picchu instead seems to have been the hub of a sizable Incan province. According to recent evidence, the city may have been built by Pachacuti, the founding patriarch of the Inca empire, and populated by his royal house. If this supposition is correct, Machu Picchu would have been constructed sometime after 1438, when Pachacuti decisively repelled enemy invaders and the Incas began expanding their empire.

Machu Picchu spans a mountain saddle between green jungle peaks. The settlement has only 200 residences, suggesting a population of about 1,000 people. Because the nearby agricultural lands could support a much larger population than this, some archaeologists theorize that the settlement's role was to grow coca leaves to send to the priests and nobility of the nearby Incan capital of Cuzco.

Left: *Machu Picchu also appears to have been a hub for religious observances. The Incas were nature worshipers, viewing as sacred whatever they saw as permeated with* huaca, *or spiritual power: rocks, peaks, rainbows, and heavenly bodies.* Opposite: *Set high on a mountain saddle in Peru, the ruins consist of temples, towers, fountains, terraces, staircases, and sites for astronomical observations. Machu Picchu seems to have been the focal point of an Inca province.*

But another idea seems to come nearer to unraveling the mysterious purpose of Machu Picchu—that it was foremost a spiritual and ceremonial center. The city contains a large number of religious buildings that were constructed with great

Seeing the skilled stone work of Machu Picchu, discoverer Hiram Bingham believed himself to be standing in the legendary final refuge of the Incas, called Vilcabamba. He was mistaken, as he was in declaring that the city had been a haven for the Inca "Virgins of the Sun."

care. One of them, the Temple of the Sun—a semicircular tower of exquisite stonework—functioned as an observatory on the heavens. A mark cut on a rock at the center of the tower lines up, through a window, with the exact spot where the sun rises on the June solstice. In the temple's recesses the Incas placed religious statues or offerings.

Another small cave at Machu Picchu served as an observatory for tracing

the December solstice. Ritual religious bathing may have been done at the Fountains, a series of 16 small waterfall baths where the sacred focus may have been water. But the principal shrine at Machu Picchu was probably the *intihuatana*—the "hitching post of the sun"—a stone that the Incas may have used to observe the heavens and mark the seasons. Every Incan settlement had such a stone, but only this one was spared destruction by Spanish conquerors, who determinedly wiped out all signs of Incan "idolatry." No one knows for certain how the stone was used.

In another part of the city, the Sacred Rock is an upright flat stone whose margin traces the outline of the mountains visible beyond it; the rock's function remains a mystery. In the Temple of the Condor, Incan artists carved a rock into the image of a condor, again for reasons unknown.

Vast terraces that edge the settlement were used for

farming and have defied the centuries. In the Royal Sector resided the community's noble members. Their spacious residences have stone lintels that weigh as much as three tons; in Inca culture these customarily set apart the residences of the powerful.

Near the settlement lie other intriguing sites. The *Intipunku*, or Sun Gate, is a notch cut in a mountain ridge that frames the rising sun during fixed periods on the calendar. The famous Inca Bridge is located along an ever-narrowing mountain trail that, at some places, is cut into a sheer cliff. The builders cleverly left a gap in a buttressed section of the trail that they could bridge with two logs. As needed, the logs could be removed to make the road impassable to outsiders.

Why did the Incas abandon Machu Picchu to the vegetation and the centuries? Among the theories: The settlement's water sources dried up, or the inhabitants were devastated by civil war, fire, or Spanish invaders.

Perhaps it is no wonder that this nearly inaccessible mountain city remained hidden and unknown to outsiders for centuries after the Incas abandoned Machu Picchu.

Easter Island Statues

Chile

The gargantuan stone figures gaze across Easter Island through eyes hooded in shadow, eyes that veil an ancient, mysterious past. The place where they stand floats alone in the South Pacific, about 2,000 miles from the coast of Chile. It is the most remote inhabited island on Earth.

The statues, called *moai,* average 23 feet tall, with the largest one measuring an incredible 69 feet. Many of the figures originally stood on stone platforms, and some wear topknots of reddish stone,

which some archaeologists believe represents a male hairstyle once common on the island. The huge topknots weigh as much as two elephants, yet they were somehow set in place atop the figures.

Scholars believe that Marquesas islanders migrated to Rapa Nui (the

island's original Polynesian name) before A.D. 400. According to local legend, however, there were two groups of early settlers—known as the Long Ears and the Short Ears—that came from different directions. It isn't clear which group carved the *moai,* but conflict between them led to the extermination of the Long Ears and damaged many monuments. Later, rival clans

No one knows exactly where Easter Island's original settlers came from or why they carved these colossal figures. The images may have represented clan ancestors.

that owned the statues toppled the *moai* to offend and anger each other. Today about 600 fallen statues lie scattered around the island. In the 20th century some were restored to their upright positions.

A number of partially carved figures still remain in the island's quarry of volcanic stone, lying horizontally, face up. Shaping even a medium-size statue probably took two teams of men at least a year. Each figure was then detached, lowered down a cliff, and somehow moved a great distance to its site—perhaps hauled on a tree-trunk sledge, transported on wooden rollers, or rolled on round stones. Finally, the immense figure had to be raised upright on an elevated platform.

Originally, the statues of Easter Island did not have the blank, empty eyes seen today, but orbs of inlaid coral and rock. Upon what lost world did they gaze?

Tuff from the island's three extinct volcanoes provided raw material for islanders to carve into the gigantic figures. The first Europeans to see the statues were a 1722 Dutch expedition that came ashore on Easter Sunday— their inspiration for naming the island.

Houses of Parliament

Standing grandly on the bank of the Thames, the Houses of Parliament trumpet the self-confidence of Victorian England in an era when the sun never set on the British Empire. Officially called the Palace of Westminster, the neo-Gothic building—whose classical symmetry contrasts with its exuberant spires and towers—takes on a storybook glow at night, when it is flooded with gold and green light.

The building rose on the foundations of a royal palace that burned almost completely in 1834. The surviving Westminster Hall dates to the 11th century, and its grand oak hammerbeam roof once sheltered the law court where Thomas More was tried. The present structure by Victorian architect Charles Barry and designer Augustus Pugin, completed in 1870, has nearly 1,200 rooms, more than two miles of corridors, and 100 staircases.

Its most famous feature is the clock tower, which houses a 13-ton bell called Big Ben. The clock itself, with a face 23 feet across, is visible from a good distance and keeps remarkably accurate time. It has faltered rarely, such as when World War II bombs shattered the clock face, and in 1949 when a flock of starlings roosted on the hands, arresting their movement.

The Houses of Parliament are, of course, the home of British government. The House of Commons occupied St. Stephen's Chapel from 1547 until the chapel was destroyed by fire in 1843. To commemorate its original home, the current House of Commons is designed so the canopied Speaker's chair looks like an altar and the benches like choir stalls. Despite the ecclesiastical ambiance of the room, debates among Members of Parliament are famous for their thoroughly secular, sharp rhetoric and passionate argumentation.

More elegantly appointed in scarlet and gold, the House of Lords has now ejected nearly all of its hereditary members. New processes for gaining membership in the House of Lords are being developed. But not even such changes as these can take away the traditional grandeur of the Houses of Parliament.

Below: *A symbol of London, the clock tower stands 320 feet high and houses Big Ben, the bell whose chimes are familiar around the world on broadcasts by the BBC World Service.* Opposite: *Filling eight acres, the Houses of Parliament reflect the opposing but compatible styles of its designers who worked together on the structure: Charles Barry brought architectural restraint while Augustus Pugin contributed his decorative exuberance.*

St. Paul's Cathedral

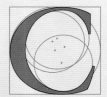 onsidered *the* church for true Londoners and the ceremonial heart of the city—this is St. Paul's. During World War II the Anglican cathedral stood through the bombs and blazes of the Blitz, giving courage to all England. Its baroque splendor has also made it a setting for great occasions in modern times, from the 1965 funeral of Winston Churchill to the wedding of Prince Charles and Lady Diana Spencer in 1981.

Four previous churches stood on the site, the earliest built in 604 at the dawn of Christianity in England. A gargantuan medieval version—the largest building in England—was a raucous haunt rife with beer sellers and beggars, ball players and rogues, market-stall vendors and their animals. In the mid-1500s authorities actually had to ban shooting inside the church.

Old St. Paul's burned in the Great Fire of London in 1666, thereby giving architect Christopher Wren an empty canvas. Protestant authorities rejected his vision of a domed baroque church of Italian style (perhaps it was too much like the Catholic St. Peter's in Rome), so he submitted a steeled design that

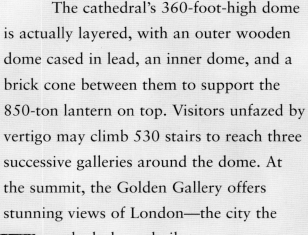

won approval. During 35 years of construction that ended in 1710, however, Wren managed through secretive tactics to add back the dome and other features of his beloved earlier plan.

The cathedral's 360-foot-high dome is actually layered, with an outer wooden dome cased in lead, an inner dome, and a brick cone between them to support the 850-ton lantern on top. Visitors unfazed by vertigo may climb 530 stairs to reach three successive galleries around the dome. At the summit, the Golden Gallery offers stunning views of London—the city the cathedral was built to serve.

Far below, in the largest crypt in Europe, tombs memorialize English heroes and artists, ranging from Admiral Lord Nelson and the Duke of Wellington to painters Joshua Reynolds and J.M.W. Turner. Cathedral architect Wren lies here too, the inscription on his tomb advising: "Reader, if you seek his monument, look around you."

Left: *As in earlier medieval cathedrals, the nave, transepts, and choir of St. Paul's form a cross. In the Whispering Gallery, about a hundred feet up inside the dome, visitors can speak softly yet be heard clearly more than 125 feet away on the opposite side of the dome. Opposite: St. Paul's Cathedral—one of more than 50 church commissions that Christopher Wren received after the London fire of 1666—ranks as England's only baroque cathedral and the first one built exclusively by one architect.*

Stonehenge

Few monuments left by a vanished people are more impressive—or more enigmatic—than Stonehenge. Archaeologists speculate that the ring of immense stones on southern England's Salisbury Plain served as an observatory to mark the seasons and as a ceremonial center to celebrate the sun. Even today during the summer solstice, you can stand at the central Altar Stone and witness the sun rising precisely over the Heel Stone, located 250 feet away. Certainly, Stonehenge was a sacred place.

Standing in the morning light like a portal to another world, the silhouetted trilithons—the structures with two vertical stones supporting a horizontal stone laid on top—only open a doorway to further questions. Who built this monument? And why?

Building began around 3000 B.C., when Neolithic people dug a circular ditch about 320 feet in diameter, using deer antlers as picks. In the second phase about 2000 B.C., a double circle of at least 60 bluestones was erected. The stones came not from nearby quarries but from Wales, 240 miles away—an amazing feat of water and overland transportation for Bronze Age people, especially

because the stones weigh four tons apiece. Available transport probably included rafts, log rollers, and sledges. Over time, though, the circles were dismantled.

Stonehenge's third phase, a century later, created the arrangement of stones whose remains we see today. The stones, hauled 20 miles from the Marlborough Downs, weighed as much as 50 tons apiece. They were set upright in a circle and topped with a continuous ring of stone lintels. Inside was a horseshoe arrangement of other trilithons. Later some of the early bluestones were erected in a horseshoe inside.

The questions about Stonehenge remain. Despite mystical notions that the Druids built Stonehenge, these Celtic people didn't reach Britain until long after the last stone was put in place. "Most of what has been written about Stonehenge is nonsense or speculation," says one eminent British archaeologist. "No one will ever have a clue what its significance was."

Left: *These massive stones were shaped by people of the Bronze Age using stone hammers the size of footballs. It probably took 600 laborers to drag one of the stones to the site. How did Bronze Age builders manage to cut, transport, and erect stones that weighed as much as 50 tons? Opposite: The largest surviving trilithon rises to a height of 21 feet. But that number still does not represent its true size, as part of its length is buried in the ground.*

Roman and Georgian Bath

Everything started around 850 B.C., or so the legend goes, when King Bladud contracted leprosy, was exiled to the English countryside, and became a swineherd. There, on the future site of Bath, he observed his itching pigs wallowing in warm, muddy springs and thereby healing their skin ailments. He followed suit—and was cured himself.

Whether this tale is fact or fancy, Romans arriving in A.D. 44 did find the local folk enjoying Bath's hot mineral waters. The Romans founded the town of Aquae Solis. Over the next four centuries, they transformed the natural hot springs into a bathing complex and a temple devoted to Sulis Minerva, the Romano-Celtic goddess of healing. The springs still feed the baths today, gushing a quarter of a million gallons of water daily at a steaming 116 degrees Fahrenheit.

The Romans left, and during the Middle Ages the town became a church center and wool market—the baths were allowed to languish. But in the early 18th century, fashionable English society began coming to Bath to "take the waters" as a health cure. A gambler named Richard "Beau" Nash became the town's master of ceremonies, the social arbiter of style and arranger of entertainments. For the smart set, Bath became the place to meet and greet, flirt, enjoy concerts and balls—and gossip.

In Georgian times Bath grew into an architectural masterpiece. A father-and-son building team, both named John Wood, used honey-hued stone from a nearby quarry to put together an elegant city whose Palladian style harked back to classical Roman days. Their famous Royal Crescent is a curving sweep of terrace houses fronted with Ionic columns. In the Assembly Rooms of 1771, creatures of fashion gathered to sip tea, play cards, and dance.

Visitors now get a taste of those days at the famously elegant Pump Room, which still serves tea while musicians play. Guests who are brave (or just historically curious) can sample the natural mineral water—which, according to one report, tastes "faintly of eggs, soap, and metal."

Opposite: For 2,000 years the reputation of Bath has come from its hot mineral springs, which have lured visitors since the era of the Romans. Their Great Bath, fed by natural hot springs, was like a huge indoor swimming pool. Its Roman paving intact but its roof gone, the bath is now open-air. Left: The Roman Baths were built about A.D. 65. Eighteen centuries later, in Georgian times, the city of Bath became a retreat for members of the fashionable set, who came to "take the waters." Jane Austen described the social scene at the posh Pump Room in her novel, Northanger Abbey.

Edinburgh Castle

Scotland

This is exactly what you would expect a Scottish castle to look like—standing high on a peak and hard as a rock, with stone walls and ramparts rising out of a volcanic crag. The foundation rock of Edinburgh Castle was cut sheer on three sides by ancient glaciers, creating a natural defensive position that has served as a fortress since the Bronze Age.

The earliest written records document the Northumbrian king Edwin building defenses on this site in the seventh century. Since then, Edinburgh Castle has been expanded and rebuilt numerous times, in accordance with the course of war and the needs of the army.

The castle dominates Edinburgh, and in turn it offers spectacular views across the city. Visitors approach on the Esplanade, a parade ground where the stirring summer Military Tattoo is performed. They enter a gate guarded by statues of Scottish resistance hero William Wallace and Robert the Bruce, whose military campaign reestablished Scotland as a separate kingdom. Above the gate is inscribed the Latin royal motto, *Nemo Me Impune Lacessit*, which can translate as, "No one attacks me and gets away with it."

Despite the castle's military atmosphere, there is also sanctity here—in a 12th-century chapel built to honor the saintly Queen Margaret, renowned for her charity to beggars. The simple, spare place of worship probably looks much as it did in her time.

History was written in the palace area of the castle, in a modest chamber where Mary, Queen of Scots, gave birth to the son who would become James VI of Scotland and James I of England. Mary came to the castle for this event because of its symbolic role as the seat (although not the residence) of Scottish royalty.

Left: *Edinburgh Castle still serves as headquarters for Britain's Scottish regiments. Within the castle walls, officers and soldiers dispatch their duties and attend bagpipers' school.* Opposite: *The castle walls encompass a military fortress, a royal residence, prisons, and a history that ranges from royal births to brutal murders. The castle also holds Europe's oldest royal regalia—the Crown, the Sceptre, and the Sword— and Edinburgh's oldest building, St. Margaret's Chapel.*

Eiffel Tower

France

As strong as iron yet as delicate as lace, the Eiffel Tower is the romantic symbol of Paris. Interestingly, its design was at first disdained by the city's artists and writers, who protested the tower's construction in 1889 for the Universal Exposition, a world's fair commemorating the 100th anniversary of the French Revolution. Eventually, however, the tower's beauty, originality, and engineering wizardry won it widespread praise and affection—as well as a place on the canvases of artists such as Pissarro and Utrillo.

Bridge engineer Gustave Eiffel designed the tower, exulting that "the French flag is the only one with a 300 meter pole." (At 984 feet, the tower ranked as the world's tallest structure for decades; modern television transmitters on top have elevated it to the present 1,063 feet.)

Eiffel's drawings were so precise, giving details for more than 18,000 metal parts, that the tower was erected in just a little more than two years. An astounding 2.5 million rivets hold the parts together, and the tower weighs in at 14.6 million pounds (7,300 tons). Repainting the tower—a job that requires 50 tons of paint—is done every seven years.

To reach the top, visitors take elevators that follow curving paths up the legs of the tower. Each year the lifts travel more than 60,000 miles. The cars need special brakes to adapt to the varying angles of descent; a crew of employees crafts replacement parts for the elevators by hand.

The tower has three platforms, and energetic visitors can tackle climbing the

Left: *Three hundred workers labored for two years to erect the tower, which proved the potential of steel construction— later used in various skyscrapers and telecommunications towers that eclipsed the tower's height.* Opposite: *The symbol of Paris—and until 1930 the tallest structure on Earth—the Eiffel Tower captures the grace of living in the French capital, a place where gardens soften the cityscape.*

stairs to the first two, reached at 187 feet and 377 feet. From the topmost platform at 899 feet, the panorama can stretch for some 50 miles on a clear day. It has been said that the streets and environs of Paris below unfold like a giant map.

Visitors reaching the top can peek into Eiffel's own salon. On their way up or down, they can choose to dine elegantly at the Jules Verne restaurant, which serves a seasonal menu of traditional French cuisine. The food nearly matches the view—and the prices definitely match the height of the tower.

Patrons look down at the green lawn known as the Champs de Mars, formerly a parade ground for the 18th-century *École Militaire,* a military academy housed in a neoclassical building at the end of the lawn. One famous graduate of the class of 1785: Napoléon.

While you're high atop the Eiffel Tower, it's comforting to know that the structure was engineered to sway no more than five inches in a strong wind. Even more remarkable, the tower actually "grows" up to nearly six inches during hot weather—a result of metal expansion.

The tower was never meant to be a permanent installation on the Paris skyline, and it was nearly dismantled in 1909. Only the emerging field of radio telegraphy saved it—antennas mounted on the tower proved vital to French transmissions. Over the decades since then, the tower has played important roles for the International Time Service, transatlantic radio telephone service, radio broadcasting, and French television.

The view from the top of the Eiffel Tower is particularly enchanting in the evening, when city lights glitter on the Seine and romance fills the air. The structure itself is lighted from within, flooded with a radiance that transforms the tower into a jewel box of silver and gold. The

A lot of criticism swirled around the tower during construction. Guy de Maupassant ridiculed it as a "high and skinny pyramid of iron ladders," while novelist Léon Bloy labeled it a "truly tragic street lamp."

The City of Light finds its loveliest expression in the Eiffel Tower by night—one of the most romantic views on Earth. Visitors seeking the best lighting conditions should ascend the tower an hour before sunset and stay as evening falls and city lights start to twinkle below.

new lights were installed as part of a major facelift the tower received in 1986 prior to the observance of its 100th birthday in 1989. A great deal of rust was removed during the work, restoring the tower to a gleaming daytime appearance as well.

Although the panorama of the city from on top can't be surpassed, the best view of the tower itself is from below. If you position yourself between the tower's feet and look up, you'll appreciate the grace of the iron latticework and see a dramatically distorted perspective of the tower soaring overhead. You'll be sharing this experience with other people from all over the world—in one year the Eiffel Tower has drawn more than six million admirers wanting to see the world-famous symbol of Paris. Its perennial popularity is assured.

Arc de Triomphe

France

The world's largest triumphal arch—measuring 164 feet high by 148 feet wide—rises at the west end of the famous Champs-Élysées. No less a figure than Napoléon commissioned the monument in 1806 to honor his own military victories. But work faltered when his armies began to suffer defeat, and the arch wasn't finished until 1836.

The Arc de Triomphe dominates Place Charles de Gaulle, which was formerly known as Place de l'Étoile because of its star shape. Baron Georges-Eugène Haussmann added seven new roads to the five that already met at the arc as part of a 19th-century revamping of Paris. Radiating from the arch, 12 avenues spread to all corners of Paris. The avenues' names commemorate generals and Napoleonic victories, a theme carried out on the arch itself. The four facades of the arch are carved in high relief with military scenes, the most celebrated being Rude's *The Departure of the Volunteers in 1792* (often called *La Marseillaise*). It shows a winged figure of the Motherland urging volunteers to battle for the nation. Other panels depict the capture of Alexandria, the Battle of Austerlitz, and similar moments of victory.

The arch itself has seen moments like these—such as General Charles de Gaulle's triumphant 1944 return to Paris—as well as defeats that still sting French pride, such as Germans marching under the arch in 1871 and Nazis goose-stepping through in 1940. Beneath the arch today lies France's Unknown Soldier, resting in a tomb where an eternal flame is symbolically rekindled each evening.

Unfortunately, visitors may go to their own tombs prematurely if they attempt to cross the manic Parisian traffic boiling around the arch. Cars eddy and spin around Place Charles de Gaulle as if whipped in a maelstrom. The arch's least interesting feature becomes most important now: a pedestrian passage beneath the street that leads to the base of the arch.

Palace of Versailles

France

The world's most opulent playground for royalty! A chateau large enough to house 6,000 courtiers! A palace fit for a king!

And not just any king, but Louis XIV, the "Sun King," who reigned for 72 years and whose self-glorification knew no bounds. Starting in 1661, he transformed a humble hunting lodge into a glittering palace. He drained swamps and moved whole forests to create 250 acres of formal gardens, tree-lined paths, flowerbeds, lakes, and fountains. And this filled only a small portion of the ground—the entire estate covered 2,000 acres.

Versailles served as France's political capital and the focal point of the court from 1682 until 1789. It was Louis XIV's motive to remove himself (and his scheming nobles) from the political intrigues of Paris, so he created a place where the court could live under his watchful eye. Its size and opulence exhibited his supreme wealth and trumpeted his power as an absolute monarch.

Building Versailles required some 30,000 laborers and was so costly that it nearly wiped out the coffers of France. The main building contains grand halls and bedrooms that interior designer Charles LeBrun decorated with every ostentatious adornment imaginable. The *Grands Appartements* of the palace are lavish showplaces filled with murals, paintings, sculptures, velvet draperies, Savonnerie carpets, gilded

When the Sun King moved into Versailles in 1682, 6,000 courtiers moved in with him. Eventually, the retinue—including nobles, staff, administrators, attendants, and the rest—swelled to 20,000 people.

bronze, and tinted marble. These salons are dedicated to Greek deities such as Hercules and Mercury. Louis XIV chose the Salon of Apollo, the sun god, to serve as the throne room for the Sun King.

Most spectacular of all is the Hall of Mirrors, a 235-foot-long drawing and ballroom lined along one side with 17 huge mirrors—fixtures that were staggeringly expensive at that time in history. In the glass the courtiers could admire their

own fabulously costumed selves as they danced. The mirrors were also designed to reflect the ceiling frescoes, which illustrate and pay tribute to the early years of Louis XIV's reign. On the other side of the room, a row of windows opened onto vast gardens and the sunset.

In the white-and-gold baroque Chapel Royal, Louis XVI wed Marie Antoinette in 1770, when both were teenagers. Among further palace additions

In 1661 Louis XIV, determined to become the envy of European royalty, had a not-to-be-outdone palace built. The finest artists spent 50 years at work on this ultimate chateau.

were a paneled library, the Clock Room (where Mozart performed at age seven), and the Opera, a huge oval theater illuminated by 10,000 candles.

Creating the gardens at Versailles required legions of workers and the genius

of landscape designer André Le Nôtre, who laid out everything in the most formal French style. The central axis of Versailles's gardens is the mile-long Grand Canal, which is situated to reflect the setting sun. Around it spread geometric expanses of plantings, flowerbeds, paths, ponds, and lakes. Not to mention fountains—some 1,400 of them at one time, including a spectacular fountain in which a horse-drawn chariot carries a triumphant Apollo—yet another reference to the glory of the Sun King.

To relieve the formal design, eccentric buildings called follies are scattered here and there—one of them a grove where the courtiers danced in summertime amid rock gardens, shells, and decorative lamps. Marble and bronze statues are arrayed along paths and tucked into the foliage. In the Orangery,

Many wars have been settled through peace talks and treaties negotiated at Versailles. The Treaty of Versailles that ended World War I was signed in the Hall of Mirrors in 1919.

3,000 trees once thrived through the winter cold.

Two smaller palaces stand on the far side of the gardens. Louis XIV built the pink marble Grand Trianon as a place to escape the relentless etiquette of court life. (In the main palace, for example, the king usually dined alone at a table in view of hundreds of onlookers. On other occasions, diners were seated in his presence in strict protocol by rank. Simply cooking for the palace's constant banquets required a kitchen staff of 2,000 people.)

The Petit Trianon was a love nest built by Louis XV, who trysted there with Madame du Barry. Later this neoclassical mini-palace found favor with Marie Antoinette, who also wanted to get away from the stiff formality she found at the main palace.

Nearby was the most charming hideaway of all—the Queen's Hamlet, a sort of play village and farm built for Marie Antoinette's amusement. Among the thatched cottages, a watermill, and a lake, she and her court acted out a fantasy of peasant life.

It is ironic, perhaps, that this same queen's lavish spending and frivolity eventually led to her royal downfall in 1789. That was when the French Revolution's mobs marched on Versailles and carried Marie Antoinette and Louis XVI away to Paris. Ultimately, in 1793, they were led to the guillotine.

Chartres Cathedral

France

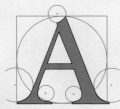 s the sun travels across the sky from dawn to twilight, the famous stained glass windows within Chartres Cathedral change colors and patterns like images in a kaleidoscope. Streams of tinted light pour across the lofty space, filling it with the glory of God.

Approaching pilgrims first spied this masterwork of 13th-century Gothic architecture as modern travelers do, soaring above the town of Chartres, its spires piercing the blue sky. Properly called the Cathédrale Notre-Dame, it was a place of pilgrimage because it houses what the faithful believe to be the veil worn by the Virgin Mary during the birth of Jesus. In 1194 the relic miraculously survived a fire that destroyed most of the earlier Romanesque cathedral on the site.

Within just 30 years that cathedral's sur-

viving elements were fleshed out with the new Gothic cathedral. Absolutely immense

at 425 feet long, the building has a nave 54 feet across, the widest in France. One of the asymmetrical bell towers is the tallest Romanesque steeple anywhere (345 feet); the other is an even loftier Gothic steeple.

The cathedral boasts 26,900 square feet of stained glass in 176 stunning windows, among them three rose windows that are world famous. The deep, intense color known as "Chartres blue" is immortalized in the cathedral's glass. Some of the windows illustrate stories from the Bible—pictures that once provided a wordless way to communicate Christian concepts to the illiterate pilgrims who flocked to the cathedral in medieval times.

On the floor of the nave lies a circular stone labyrinth. Although the

During World Wars I and II, all of the cathedral's 176 stained glass windows were removed, piece by piece, and stored away for protection. The three rose windows each measure nearly 44 feet across.

labyrinth measures only 42 feet across, its looping path would extend for 856 feet if it were unwound. The labyrinth has long served the faithful as a symbolic pilgrimage to the Holy Land and as a mystical walking meditation. Indeed, Chartres Cathedral has enough beauty and sanctity to satisfy any pilgrim.

One of Europe's greatest examples of Gothic architecture, Chartres Cathedral employs flying buttresses to brace the walls. Spared major alteration over the centuries, the cathedral maintains a rare architectural unity.

Mont-St.-Michel

France

agnificent Mont-St.-Michel rises out of a bay, an abbey perched on a pinnacle of rock. Dramatically silhouetted against the sky of Normandy, it is one of Europe's greatest religious edifices.

The granite outcrop lies several hundred yards offshore. Depending on the positions of the moon and sun, the difference in sea level between low and high tide here can be an astonishing 45 feet. When the tide is out, the Mont is surrounded by a sandy expanse that extends for miles. But when the tide shifts roughly six hours later, the incoming water rushes across the flat floor of the bay at the speed, according to legend, of a galloping horse. (Actually, the pace is closer to a person walking quickly.) Unwary visitors have been caught by the racing seawater or trapped in perilous patches of quicksand—the same hazards that once endangered medieval pilgrims coming to the abbey.

In the eighth century construction began here after Aubert, the bishop of Avranches, beheld a vision of the Archangel Michael that inspired him to build a devotional chapel. Three centuries later began the improbable feat of building an abbey on the 264-foot-high summit of rock, a labor that lasted half a millennium.

The abbey housed increasingly powerful Benedictine monks and, having just one opening in the ramparts, has been described as an ecclesiastical fortress. Mont-St.-Michel was the only place in this region of France to withstand English assault during the Hundred Years' War.

The monastic buildings, known as *La Merveille* ("The Wonder"), include the abbey church, a winning hodgepodge of architecture with a Romanesque nave and a choir of Flamboyant Gothic style. It is topped with a gilded figure of the Archangel Michael. Exquisitely carved arches set on pink granite columns line the cloister.

How did the stones needed to build this amazing abbey get here? They were brought from nearby quarries in boats, then hauled up the steep slope by ropes and sheer human strength. The mighty labor took centuries—and paid off beautifully.

Opposite: *Mont-St.-Michel experiences the highest tide differential on the European continent. Over the centuries, pilgrims trying to make their way to the abbey sometimes drowned in the incoming tide or were trapped in patches of quicksand.* Below: *Guy de Maupassant called Mont-St.-Michel "the most wonderful Gothic dwelling ever made for God on this earth ... a gigantic granite jewel, which is as delicate as a piece of lacework." The abbey was built between the 11th and 16th centuries.*

THE
Alhambra

Spain

Travelers for centuries have been mesmerized by the Alhambra—a Moorish fantasy palace of domes and pointed arches, shady patios and gleaming tiles. Everywhere is the sound of water, a rare treasure in arid Spain. Splashing into fountains, meandering through graceful channels, water was made an art form here—the equal of the woodwork, ornate plaster, and ceramic tile of the palace itself.

The best preserved medieval Muslim palace in the world, the Alhambra was built in the 13th and 14th centuries by the Nasrid kings. Of the early Alcazaba, or fortress, little remains but hulking red ramparts and a

To supply the Alhambra with water for fountains and pools, the Nasrid king Ibn al-Ahmar diverted the River Darro to the palace hill. The style of the Alhambra reflects the Moors, who occupied Granada.

bell tower overlooking the fabled city of Granada. What hypnotizes travelers is the exquisitely refined royal palace. Its stucco walls are carved with graceful Arabic calligraphy or sheathed in rich tile mosaics. The 50-foot-high domed ceiling of one royal salon is intricately inlaid with more than 8,000 pieces of cedarwood and designed to represent the firmament.

Visitors first pass through public rooms where the sultans received visitors. Farther inside lie private quarters that were open only to the sultan, his family, harem, and servants (most of them eunuchs, to reduce their interest in the harem). The women enjoyed the Court of the Lions, whose 12 stone beasts spurt water that fills a pool and flows into channels branching off to nearby rooms.

In the Hall of the Abencerrajes, plaster resembling lace hanging from the ceiling like stalactites and star-shaped cupola reflect in a pool. Elsewhere the sultan's

Above: *The arched gallery of the Patio of the Lions is held aloft by 124 delicate marble columns. Here one finds the feeling of a medieval cloister blended with an Asian atmosphere.* Opposite: *One of Spain's most popular places to visit, the Alhambra has three parts: the old fortress, or Alcazaba; the magnificent royal palace; and the shaded Generalife gardens. They are located atop La Sabika hill, overlooking Granada.*

favorites would pamper themselves in the colorfully tiled royal baths—as the sultan observed from the balcony and chose his companion for the evening.

Adjacent to the palace is the Generalife, where one of Spain's finest gardens spellbinds viewers with sprays of water, terraces of roses, lily ponds, bowers, shrubs trimmed like crenellated castle walls, and shady cypress trees. Like the Alhambra palace itself, the garden floats you far away from the 21st century.

Guggenheim Museum, Bilbao

Spain

World-famous architect Philip Johnson called it "the greatest building of our time." It is "a miracle," said *The New York Times*. Certainly, few buildings in history have generated so much praise or have so greatly changed a city as Frank Gehry's museum on the industrial riverfront of Bilbao.

The city, once the culturally moribund commercial center of Spain's Basque region, was revitalized by the 1997 opening of this radically unconventional museum—an irregular fusion of limestone, glass, and a shell of thousands of lustrous titanium sheets. Admirers have compared the museum to a titanium clipper ship under full sail (harking back to Bilbao's shipbuilding history) and to a spaceship from Alpha Centauri (underlining the museum's futuristic look, an apt setting for its collection of contemporary art). To one Spanish novelist, the blaze of titanium and light is a "meteorite."

Critics, on the other hand, have described the museum as looking like a cauliflower or a large soufflé. In any case, few visitors remain unmoved upon entering the museum's 150-foot-high atrium, from which glass elevators and metal walkways lead to 19 exhibition spaces—including the world's largest gallery, measuring 426 feet long and 98 feet wide. The ground-floor galleries suit large-scale artworks and installations, and some pieces were specifically made to fit their exhibit spaces, among them Richard Serra's *Serpent*.

Works of art displayed at "El Guggy" come from New York's Solomon R. Guggenheim Museum and from the Basque government. Pieces range from abstract expressionist to cubist and geometrical, and include many big names of 20th-century art: Kandinsky, Picasso, Pollock, De Kooning.

Still, the museum itself remains the main attraction. Visitors gaze out through tall windows, running their eyes along the museum's titanium ripples. They've never seen anything like *this* before!

Below: *Once known for shipbuilding, Bilbao is now famous for its art museum. A futuristic vision set in an old industrial district, the Guggenheim almost instantly transformed this commercial city into a cultural center.*
Opposite: *Many visitors come not to see the works of art, but for the museum itself. The exterior is sheathed in 30,000 titanium panels that have been compared to the scales of a fish—a sea creature that has often inspired architect Frank Gehry.*

THE
Colosseum

The Colosseum proclaimed the greatness of the Roman Empire, and even today its ruins are so impressive we almost forget that the arena was built for a terrible purpose—as a place where men and animals were slaughtered for the amusement of the crowd.

The Colosseum was a remarkable feat of engineering by people who lived more than 2,000 years ago. The building itself was 615 feet long and 510 feet wide.

With the walls standing 159 feet tall, it held as many as 55,000 spectators. To efficiently direct the huge throng into the arena, each spectator was given a token indicating which of the stadium's 80 arched entrances to use and which seat to

take. The entire crowd could enter and exit very quickly. Spectators were shielded from the roasting Mediterranean sun by the remarkable *velarium*—a huge awning roped to masts along the building's upper story. It resembled a ship's sails, and, in fact, sailors worked the canvas.

Beneath the stadium floor a maze of chambers and cages held condemned prisoners and wild animals. Manual-powered elevators lifted the cages to a level where the animals could escape—but only through a trapdoor into the arena. At the Colosseum's opening in A.D. 80, bloodthirsty spectators enjoyed the slaughter of 5,000 animals.

During the "games," criminals and Christians were regularly thrown to the lions. To absorb the spilled blood, the arena's wooden floor was covered with sand. (*Arena* means "sandy place" in Latin.) But

During the "games," the emperor, his family, and priestesses called the Vestal Virgins sat in ringside boxes. Above them in sloping tiers of marble seats sat important citizens, then the middle class, then slaves and foreigners. The hot upper reaches of the stadium were for women and the poor.

gladiatorial combat was the main event. Combatants paraded into the arena, bowing before the emperor to shout: "We who are about to die salute you!" Indeed, half of the gladiators could count on being killed that day.

Since the era of the gladiators, the Colosseum has fallen to ruin. Earthquakes took a toll, Renaissance palace builders used it as a source of building materials, and modern Rome's air pollution is blackening the stadium with soot that eats away at the stone. Efforts are underway to restore the great monument—a propitious move, because an old proverb warns: "When the Colosseum falls, Rome also ends, and when Rome falls, the world will end."

A majestic sight to this day, the Roman Colosseum stands more than 150 feet high. The Romans were able to build high walls that wouldn't cave in under their own weight by employing open arches (rather than solid stone) and by building with concrete, a material they developed.

THE
Pantheon

With its remarkable dome, the Pantheon ranks as one of the great architectural marvels of ancient Rome. The building derives its beauty and harmony from its geometrical purity. Like an orange cut in half, the dome is a hemisphere. Unlike a halved orange, though, it is perfect: The dome's diameter is precisely the same as its height from the floor at about 142 feet.

In the center of the dome, a round eye opens to the sky. This oculus, an aperture measuring 27 feet across, admits a stream of sunlight—the building's only source of illumination. During shadow and storm, the oculus reveals oddly beautiful special effects in the celestial fragment that appears.

Opposite: The Pantheon's dome is an architectural marvel. It was by far the largest dome built up until its time in the second century, and its size was not surpassed for 1,300 years. Right: Although the Pantheon's exterior may get most of the attention, its interior houses many treasures of its own. All lighting is natural, entering through the 27-foot oculus in the dome.

The hole seems to connect the Pantheon to the sky and stars above—an impression that is only fitting, as the building was dedicated to Rome's planetary deities. Completed around A.D. 120, the Pantheon was rededicated as a Christian church some 500 years later. This move no doubt helped to protect the site and probably explains why the Pantheon is the most complete and best-preserved building from imperial Rome.

The Pantheon's original bronze doors still survive, standing 24 feet high. In Roman days the interior was richly decorated. Niches held figures of deities, and a statue of Jupiter, Rome's primary god, stood in the center, illuminated at noon by a shaft of light from the oculus overhead.

The ancient dome is literally superlative: the largest cast-concrete construction on Earth until the 20th century. (At 142 feet across, it beats the dome of St. Peter's Basilica by six feet.) But how is the whole thing supported? No arches show, because they were embedded inside the 20-foot-thick walls, where they function like buttresses. And the dome's weight was reduced by using hollow, decorative coffering inside.

It is no wonder that the Pantheon, a surviving remnant of a world long vanished, still inspires architects to this day.

St. Peter's Basilica and the Sistine Chapel

The front entrance to St. Peter's Basilica is an enormous piazza framed by two long, curving colonnades—a design that symbolizes the arms of the Roman Catholic church reaching out to embrace the faithful. The piazza can hold some 300,000 people with room to spare.

From there the crowds enter the basilica, whose sumptuously decorated interior sprawls under a towering dome designed by Michelangelo. The huge edifice, the worldwide center of the Roman Catholic faith, was erected on what is believed to be the site of the tomb of Saint Peter, replacing a ruined basilica built by Constantine in the fourth century.

Work on the new building began in 1506 and continued for well over a century.

To prove this is the "world's biggest church," the nave is laid with gilded bronze markers to indicate the lengths of other cathedrals. The interior here extends 615 feet, with 11 chapels and 45 altars.

At the center of the church a canopy of gilded bronze, resting atop 66-foot-high spiraling columns, shelters the high altar where only the Pope may celebrate mass. Bernini designed the canopy—a curlicued Baroque extravaganza.

A highlight among the basilica's artistic treasures, Michelangelo's *Pietà* is a heartbreakingly expressive portrayal of Mary with the lifeless body of Jesus draped across her lap. Michelangelo sculpted the marble statue when he was just 25 years old, and it was the only piece he ever signed.

In the nearby Vatican Palace, the Sistine Chapel displays one of the world's

Bernini's baldacchino, *or altar canopy, was made from bronze plundered from Rome's Pantheon in 1633. The canopy is situated directly above the legendary tomb of St. Peter, said to be located in an old necropolis below the basilica.*

Above: *Considering himself a sculptor, Michelangelo viewed painting the Sistine Chapel ceiling as a chore. But Pope Julius II pressed him into service to create the frescoes, which cover over 1,000 square yards. The ceiling is so arresting that some visitors ignore the side walls, painted by Italian Renaissance masters such as Botticelli. Opposite: St. Peter's is so huge that it can hold 60,000 people. Visitors can climb within the dome—which soars 390 feet above the high altar—to the top lantern for an unparalleled vista of Rome.*

most famous artworks—the Biblical ceiling frescoes that took Michelangelo four years to complete. On the chapel's altar wall at the end of the building, Michelangelo created the masterful *Last Judgment*, depicting souls of the dead rising to meet God. The expansive theme resonates perfectly with the scale and purpose of St. Peter's.

Pompeii

Like an insect frozen in amber, Pompeii preserves a moment of the past for people who came long afterward. The city was sealed like a time capsule when the eruption of mighty Mount Vesuvius buried it under ash and volcanic pumice stone in A.D. 79. Today we can, in effect, step back nearly 2,000 years into the Greco-Roman world. Strolling through the excavated streets, we can wander into houses decorated with colorful frescoes, glance into shops, admire a 5,000-seat theater, and even read the bawdy graffiti scrawled on walls. Archaeologists have uncovered statues and mosaics, unearthed household objects, and found the bodies of people tragically killed in the midst of their daily chores.

Founded in the seventh century B.C., Pompeii came successively under Greek and Roman power, growing into a prosperous trading port of 20,000 people. Only 10 percent of its people died in the eruption; the majority had fled, heeding the rumblings and dark warning clouds emitted by the volcano.

After the cataclysm of A.D. 79, the town lay buried and unknown until the 18th century. Excavations began in 1748, and today the Italian sun shines down on the ruins of villas, baths, and temples—all signs of Pompeii's affluence. Houses had central atriums to let in light and air, and they stood along well-paved streets. The pavement in front of the House of the Faun is inscribed with the earliest known "welcome mat," while the House of the Vetii preserves paintings on mythological themes.

Via dell'Abbondanza was Pompeii's "Main Street," where bakeries, wine shops, and grocers did business. The walls are painted with notices of upcoming games and pitches for political candidates. If this resembles the daily life of today, perhaps the lesson of Pompeii is that the more things change, the more they stay the same.

Opposite: Ironically, Pompeii was built on an earlier lava flow from Vesuvius, the looming volcano that has erupted hundreds more times since the disaster of A.D. 79. In 1631 the volcano killed thousands of people, and it last erupted in 1944. Volcanologists still classify Vesuvius as active. Right: The House of Menander (named for a Greek playwright) was one of Pompeii's most elaborately decorated residences, with paintings adorning the walls and a small niche devoted to household gods.

THE
Leaning Tower of Pisa

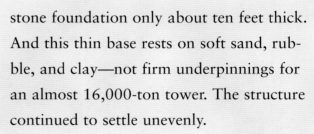

One of the world's most recognizable buildings is surely the Leaning Tower of Pisa. Go see it, if you're so inclined....

Tourists stand in front of the tipsy tower, leaning at a jaunty angle themselves, and take snapshots in which they seem to disobey the laws of gravity. In fact, people have been having fun with the tower's tilt for centuries. When construction of this campanile began in 1173, Pisa was a trading center at the peak of its military might and artistic achievement. Much to the embarrassment of Pisans, however, their white marble tower began to tilt even before its third story was finished in 1274.

Opposite: *The white marble tower was designed as a complement to Pisa's cathedral. As the tower began to tilt, Italians dubbed it the* Torre Pendente *(leaning tower). No one thinks it is possible to straighten the tower, or wants to see it upright—especially Pisa's tourist industry.*
Right: *The tower's exterior is ringed with graceful arcades, the arches supported by 190 marble and granite columns. Galileo climbed to the top of the tower to conduct his historic experiments on gravity and the velocity of falling objects.*

Perhaps engineer Bonanno Pisano failed to consider the consequences of designing a 185-foot-tall tower with a

stone foundation only about ten feet thick. And this thin base rests on soft sand, rubble, and clay—not firm underpinnings for an almost 16,000-ton tower. The structure continued to settle unevenly.

Nonetheless, construction continued. To make up for the tilt, builders made each new tier a little taller on the short side—but the additional stone only made the tower sink more. Upon completion in 1350, the tower was leaning a full 4 feet, 7 inches from vertical.

Up in the belfry, the weight of the bells caused the structure to tilt still farther. By the late 20th century the tower was leaning more than 17 feet toward the south, and a rescue operation was begun. Engineers removed soil from under the north side of the tower to even out the differences in the foundation. During the restoration, visitors were not allowed to enter the tower and climb the 293-step spiral staircase to the top. The lean was reduced by more than 15 inches. Hard to believe? What less would you expect for a tower standing on what Pisans call the *Campo dei Miracoli*—the Field of Miracles.

St. Mark's Basilica

Its shadowy, mysterious interior gleams with treasures—golden mosaics, colored marbles, emeralds, and pearls—making St. Mark's one of Europe's most glorious and exotic cathedrals. Because it is Byzantine in style and holds riches that a powerful Venetian state looted from Constantinople, St. Mark's has been called a "glittering robbers' den, the only church in Christendom that would not look out of place in Xanadu."

Consecrated in 1094, the basilica is surely Venice's holiest shrine—beneath the high altar rest the mortal remains of Saint Mark the Evangelist. These bones were another prize of plunder, stolen in 828 from their tomb in Alexandria, Egypt. Venice declared Saint Mark the city's patron saint and enshrined his bones in an earlier basilica on the same site. When that church was destroyed by fire in 976, Saint Mark's remains were thought lost. But in the 11th century, it is said, the Evangelist miraculously reappeared during mass at the new basilica, thrusting his hand out of a pillar.

The building is laid out like a Greek cross, with five bulging domes and five arched entrances. Its most famous treasure stands behind the altar in the sanctuary—the *Pala d'Oro,* a golden altar screen encrusted with jewels. Fabricated in Constantinople for the doge in 976, it was later embellished by Venetian goldsmiths. In the basilica's treasury lie more riches, primarily looted from Constantinople but in turn diminished themselves over time by plundering and sell-offs to raise funds.

The church's museum houses a team of four gilded bronze horses that for centuries stood proudly atop St. Mark's as emblems of Venice and its unrestrained power. Due to the dangers from modern air pollution, these originals have been moved inside, replaced outside by replicas. The horses look so natural that Petrarch

For centuries, St. Mark's served as the private chapel of the doges and was used on state occasions. After 1075 every Venetian trader returning from the East was ordered to bring a treasure to ornament the building. It became the city's cathedral in 1807.

said he expected them to "neigh and stamp their feet." Spoils of the Fourth Crusade in 1204, the team is said to have come from Constantinople's Hippodrome, an ancient racecourse.

St. Mark's Basilica—filled with artworks that glitter like treasure in the perpetual twilight of the interior—continues to delight the world with the storybook spell of Xanadu itself.

The basilica mingles the decorative styles of East and West into an Asian fantasy of domes, mosaics, glittering jewels, and carvings. Mostly Byzantine, the design was inspired by the Church of the Twelve Apostles in Constantinople. Of five portals, the central one is elaborately carved in Romanesque style.

Neuschwanstein Castle

Germany

Turrets and spires, winding stairways and carved wooden chambers, even a golden chandelier—Neuschwanstein has everything you could hope for in a fairy-tale castle. (So much so, in fact, that Walt Disney seems to have borrowed heavily from the design for his Sleeping Beauty Castle at Disneyland.)

An architectural fantasy created by "Mad" King Ludwig II, it perches on a forested knoll above a lake, and its theatrical appearance is no accident. Ludwig blasted away part of a mountain peak for the castle's dramatic setting and worked on the drawings with a stage designer rather than an architect. Starting work in 1869, the king yearned to create a dreamlike castle and also to evoke the atmosphere of the Wagnerian operas he loved.

Fourteen laborers spent nearly five years just carving the woodwork in the king's chamber, including an elaborate bed canopy and panels fashioned to look like Gothic windows. A mural portrays the legend of Tristan and Isolde—one of the castle's many painted scenes from the myths that inspired Wagner's operas.

Ludwig's romantic extravagance is on view everywhere: columns sculpted to resemble palm trees, a royal study where the only fabric used is hand-embroidered

silk, a floor made with 2.5 million pieces of marble, and a gilded chandelier that weighs nearly one ton—not to mention an artificial grotto with stalactites and a rushing waterfall. The windows in the castle frame views that are like pages from a storybook, complete with dark woods, mist-shrouded lakes, and majestic peaks.

To build Neuschwanstein Castle, Ludwig paid out a fortune—his own as well as the state's. To stop the lavish spending, his alarmed ministers eventually had the king declared insane and removed him from the throne. A few days later, Ludwig drowned himself, and his fairy-tale castle remained unfinished. The monarch had spent only a few months there, living out his romantic dreams.

Left: *Neuschwanstein was the least costly of Ludwig's three castles, with a price tag of "only" 6.2 million gold marks. Over the years, however, the admission fees paid by tourists have more than repaid the castle's cost and later upkeep.* Opposite: *Featured on countless calendars and tourist brochures, Neuschwanstein was the fantasy of King Ludwig II, inspired by romantic German legends and the splendor of Versailles. The "mad" king was not insane, though there was madness in his family: His aunt believed she had eaten a grand piano made of glass.*

THE
Kremlin and Red Square

Russia

With nearly a dozen palaces and churches, the Kremlin is a living repository of eight centuries of Russia's history and culture, not to mention an emblem of its power. The Kremlin walls—running almost a mile and a half, standing as high as 62 feet, as thick as 21 feet in places—include 20 towers and gates. Even with all those entrances, over the years the Kremlin has created a stronghold for the czars, a command center for the Communist party, and today a home for the Russian president.

In Russian, the word *kreml* means "citadel," and many Russian cities have kremlins of their own. The Moscow Kremlin began as a wooden fortification, built in 1156 by a prince who chose a strategic site where the Moskow and Neglinnaya rivers meet. Many of the cathedrals and palaces—those that seem the very essence of Russia, that create an

enchanted fairy-tale atmosphere—were begun three-and-a-half centuries later, when Ivan III brought in architects from Italy. These foreign designers mingled domestic Russian styles and imported Renaissance ideas to create the light, airy Cathedral of the Assumption, the Palace of Facets, and the Kremlin's distinctive brick walls and towers.

Facing the oldest square in Moscow, the Cathedral of the Assumption is the Kremlin's main church. Beneath its golden domes, czars were crowned. Frescoes cover walls that were gilded first to suggest the look of an illuminated manuscript. Priceless icons from as long ago as the 15th century gleam in the soft light. Ivan the Terrible's wooden throne of 1551 reposes in all its elaborately carved splendor. Chapels hold the tombs of every leader of the Russian church up to the Soviet era.

Opposite: Topped by the Ivan the Great Bell Tower—once the tallest building in Moscow—the Kremlin is a jewel box of palaces and cathedrals that reflect eight centuries of Russian life and history. Right: Walled for defense, the Kremlin first took shape as a fortress in the 12th century. It has sheltered Russian rulers, religious leaders, the French (who occupied it in 1812), and the Soviet government.

On vast Red Square stands St. Basil's Cathedral (1560), whose onion domes seem to say "Russia," and the Lenin Mausoleum, completed six years after the Bolshevik Party leader's death in 1924.

Near the cathedral rises the octagonal Ivan the Great Bell Tower, more than 265 feet high and at one time the tallest structure in Moscow. In the adjacent belfry hang 21 bells, the biggest of which always tolled three times to announce the death of the czar. On a granite base outside sits the 200-ton Czar Bell, the world's largest bell, although it has never been rung. A large chunk of it cracked off when a fire swept through the foundry and cold water was thrown upon the searing bronze bell.

The Armory is now a museum, displaying not only weapons from the Kremlin workshops but also the great treasures of Russia. The incalculable wealth gathered by princes and czars includes, of course, the famous Fabergé eggs, created by Gustav Fabergé and his son for the Romanov family. Lavishly decorated and bejeweled, the eggs contain surprises such as mechanical singing birds, blooming flowers, and even a tiny Trans-Siberian railroad train that, when wound up with a golden key, actually moves.

The Armory also exhibits carriages, clothing, and jewels, including Catherine the Great's gilded summer carriage, her elaborately embroidered coronation dress, and her scepter topped with the 190-carat Orlov diamond. The diamond was a gift from her lover, Count Orlov, and was originally taken from an idol's eye in an Indian temple. Among the thrones—made of carved ivory, decorated with precious stones, and all manner of wonders—is that of Peter the Great, which includes a secret compartment where his half-sister used to conceal herself and whisper advice on matters of state.

The Kremlin is itself a collection of sorts, embracing several palaces. The Terem Palace appears to have been wafted from a fairy tale, a wondrous fabrication with a red-and-white checkered roof and 11 golden onion domes. It was built in 1635 and 1636 for Czar Mikhail Romanov, whose royal bedchamber only he, his wife, and blind storytellers were allowed to enter. The Renaissance-style Palace of Facets, named for the stonework on its façade, boasts a vaulted hall once used as the throne room and banqueting chamber of the czars.

Both of these palaces were integrated into the gargantuan Great Kremlin Palace. Commissioned by Czar Nicholas I in 1837, it has 700 rooms and enormous ceremonial halls. The walls of St. George's Hall glow with the gold-inscribed names of men decorated by the military, while its six chandeliers blaze with 3,000 lightbulbs. The hall hosts diplomatic receptions and solemn ceremonies, as in 1961 when cosmonaut Yury Gagarin received the Golden Star Hero Award here. In 1994 Queen Elizabeth II of Britain met with president Boris Yeltsin in another stunning chamber, tinted cream and gold, that once served as Catherine the Great's throne room.

If the Kremlin represents the private, hidden side of Russian power, Red Square, immediately east of the Kremlin, is its public face. Dating from the late 15th century, the square was built shortly after the completion of the Kremlin walls, and the two have been joined in the popular imagination ever since. *Krasnaya Ploshchad,* as it is called in Russian, was originally separated from the Kremlin by a moat, which was ultimately paved over in 1812. It has seen more than its share of celebrations and riots, but today it might be most commonly remembered as the site of Soviet May Day and October Revolution Day parades, when the stone-faced Soviet leadership famously reviewed all their most-up-to-date military hardware.

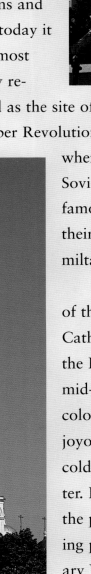

At the south end of the square sits the Cathedral of St. Basil the Blessed, built in the mid-16th century. Its colorful domes present a joyous contrast to the cold, gray Moscow winter. Lenin's Mausoleum, the purported final resting place for revolutionary Vladimir I. Lenin,

Above: *With nine gilded domes, the Kremlin's Cathedral of the Annunciation—built in 1490 as the private church of the royal family—is warmly decorated inside, from its jasper floors to a stunning painting of Christ Pantocrator in the cupola.* Left: *The Ivan the Great Belltower was named "Ivan" because it replaced a church erected by Ivan I, and called the "Great" for its height. It stands beside the Assumption Belfry, which dates to 1543. Its largest bell, cast with melted metal from older bells, rang for important state occasions.*

sits adjacent to the Kremlin walls. The long lines of viewers waiting to take a peak at the former Soviet leader's remains have dissipated since the fall of the Soviet Union, but there are always some curious souls queued up at the entrance.

Russian history continues to weave variations, lacing and entwining the palaces, cathedrals, and golden domes both inside and outside the Kremlin walls.

THE
Parthenon and the Acropolis

Greece

Suppose a postage stamp were issued to commemorate the birthplace of democracy and western culture. What picture would be chosen for it? Very likely it would be a view of the Acropolis, the hill where the graceful, white Parthenon rises against the blue sky of Greece. This temple dates to the fifth century B.C., and even today, with the smog of modern Athens around it, the Parthenon radiates purity and perfection—qualities that define the Greek classical age.

Made up of limestone and red schist, the Acropolis and its slopes were inhabited as long as 5,000 years ago, during the Bronze Age. In Mycenaean times the Acropolis was built up with fortifications, a palace, and temples. Eventually the 300-foot-high rock became the hub of the ascendant city-state of Athens.

The sanctuaries of the Acropolis were demolished when the Persians sacked Athens, but a few years later Pericles undertook a vast public works program, with the Parthenon as his first major project. He intended the Parthenon to be an awe-inspiring landmark, and it would soon be renowned all over the ancient world. For its construction Pericles hired the sculptor Phidias, who supervised a team of architects and artists that started work in 447 B.C.

The resulting temple honored the virgin goddess Athena, and in the dim light of her cult chamber stood a wooden-frame statue at least 35 feet tall, adorned with ivory and gold plate. The figure was draped with bracelets, charms, and other decorations, her eyes were precious gems, and on her breast was an ivory gorgon's head. Athena's priestesses were given a spe-

Left: *The Parthenon embodies the principles that raised Greek architecture to perfection— harmony, proportion, elegance, grace. More than 150 years ago, Charles Garnier wrote: "Sit on the threshold of the Parthenon . . . and you will remain there for hours, gazing at the same columns again and again." Opposite: The plateau of the Acropolis stretches for 1,000 feet, creating a perfect platform for the Parthenon. Phidias, who oversaw construction on the Acropolis in the fifth century B.C., also sculpted the statue of Zeus at Olympia, one of the Seven Wonders of the Ancient World.*

cial room in the temple; in fact, the word *Parthenon* means "virgin's chamber."

If the goddess Athena represented virgin purity, so too did her white marble temple radiate a perfection never before achieved in human works. The Parthenon was designed by architects Ictinus and Callicrates according to the dictates of the

Like the Parthenon, the Erechtheion once had a roof and a coffered marble ceiling. In 1801 Lord Elgin made off with a caryatid from the porch, a prize he sold to the British Museum. Today, Greece wants the "Elgin Marbles" and other ancient treasures returned home.

Doric order—familiar to college students everywhere as employing fluted columns with a plain top and round molding at the top. Within this style, the Parthenon attains a harmony that nearly surpasses understanding. The structure's pleasing proportions derive from the ratio 9:4, a mathematical ideal that informs the relationships of length to width, width to height, and the space between columns as compared to their diameters.

All the apparently straight lines of the Parthenon are, in truth, slightly

curved—but the architects knew these lines would give the impression of being correctly linear. To compensate for the eye's tendency to see a column as thinner in the middle, the designers bowed each column. The columns were also slanted inward slightly. In a final refinement, the columns at the temple's corners were made thicker, since they catch more sunlight than other columns and so would appear thinner unless the architects compensated.

Plutarch said of the temple project: "The monuments were imposing in their

Left: *All the female statues that serve as columns in the porch of the Erechtheion are replicas. Five of the originals were removed for display in the Acropolis Museum to protect them from the air pollution of Athens; the sixth was looted by Elgin. Below: In classical Greece the Parthenon was difficult to see clearly from below, due to the other buildings and statues jam-packed onto the Acropolis. Today the Parthenon stands in simple relief atop the bare ancient hill.*

Another building, the Propylaea, served as the formal entrance to the Acropolis. The architect Mnesicles ingeniously designed it with commanding stone columns on the outside to impress and inspire people as they arrived at the hill. Visitors today can still see a bit of the original coffered ceiling, which was painted and gilded.

The Parthenon itself was also originally painted, almost gaudily, in red, blue, and gold. What a postage stamp picture *that* would make!

unrivaled grandeur, beauty, and grace; the artists vied with one another in the technical perfection of their work, but the most admirable thing was the speed of execution." Building the Parthenon took only nine years, a remarkable achievement.

Considered even more sacred than the Parthenon, the nearby Erechtheion was the last of Pericles' great projects on the Acropolis, and it reconciled the worship of Athena with that of the city's early patron, Poseidon-Erectheus. In Greek mythology, Poseidon struck the ground here with his trident and created a saltwater spring, whereas Athena caused an olive tree to spring up from a rock. A serpent-king appointed by Zeus as judge determined that Athena had made the earlier claim, and that

in any case olives were more valuable than saltwater. Thus, Poseidon had to go halves on the shrine, accepting the role of Athena.

Built about 420 B.C., the Erechtheion is an Ionic temple divided into two sections—one for Athena, one for Poseidon—beautified with garland, palm, and lotus ornamentations. The most celebrated element, though, is the Porch of the Caryatids, in which columns were replaced by statues of maidens in tunics.

Hagia Sophia

Turkey

When it was consecrated in 537, no one in the history of architecture had attained the sophistication or shown the daring to erect such a building. The interior of the church—so vast that huge crowds of people could fit inside—is topped by a dome that seems suspended from the sky. Supported on four freestanding piers, the dome soars 183 feet above the floor, while soft light from high windows adds to the impression of immense, airy space. This is Hagia Sophia, or *Ayasofya* in Turkish—the church whose name means, literally, Divine Wisdom.

It was built as an imperial church by Justinian the Great, who insisted on using rare materials such as marble panels and breccia columns. In 1453, when its city of Constantinople fell to the Muslim Ottomans, Hagia Sophia's fate changed; it was converted to a mosque and dedicated to Allah. The Ottomans added a prayer niche called a mihrab that points the faith-

Right: Serving as a church for a millennium, then a mosque, and now a museum, Hagia Sophia is one of the world's great architectural creations and the finest Byzantine building in Istanbul. Its design, with a lofty dome and glittering mosaics, was meant to mirror the heavens. Opposite: Hagia Sophia influenced and inspired architects for centuries after its consecration in 537. The width of its dome was equaled only a thousand years later, when Michelangelo designed the dome of St. Peter's in Rome.

ful toward Makkah, a screened loge for the sultan, and, hanging above the nave, huge wooden plaques inscribed with Arabic calligraphy. Outside, they attached four minarets.

The Muslims also covered the church's exquisite figurative mosaics with whitewash, a covering that preserved many of them until the structure was renovated in the 13th century. Among Hagia Sophia's mosaics, the real conversation piece is one depicting Empress Zoe and her husband,

Constantine IX—whose face was the third to fill the same space, as each of the empress's consorts was replaced. One particularly lovely design of Christ, the Virgin, and John the Baptist dates to the 1300s, a last flaring of the Byzantine spirit. The emperors Constantine and Justinian appear in another scene, handing over Istanbul and Hagia Sophia to the Virgin and Child.

So—is Hagia Sophia a church or a mosque? Kemal Ataturk, who founded the Turkish Republic, ended that debate by declaring Hagia Sophia a national museum in 1935. Today, its glory is open to all.

Krak des Chevaliers

Syria

This Crusader castle in Syria, fortified in the second half of the 12th century, reveals a form perfectly suited to its function—in this case, defense against siege. The castle's surrounding curtain wall encloses a second ring of walls and towers built around a central court. With this concentric layout, the knights could defend the outer perimeter from Muslim attackers and then fall back, if need be, toward the center. Because the inner walls are higher than the outer, the defenders could always dominate their enemy from a superior height.

To further thwart attackers, the Crusaders (known as Knights Hospitallers) built a great stone slope against the castle's slightly vulnerable south side. Eighty feet thick at the base, this masonry slope was so smooth that Lawrence of Arabia, who attempted to scale it barefoot in 1909, could only make it halfway up. (And that was without any knights bombarding him with stones and boiling oil.)

Other castle features that obstructed assailants include a moat, a drawbridge, and a steep passageway with four gates and an iron grating that slid down from the ceiling, closing a passageway completely. A series of zigzags forced invaders to move slowly, while strategic openings overhead allowed knights to shower their enemy with arrows, rocks, and flaming pitch.

Withstanding numerous Arab assaults during their more than 100 years of occupation, the knights lived securely within the castle. The interior precincts have a fine Gothic balcony, a banqueting hall, a plain 12th-century Romanesque chapel, a stable that still has loops on the wall for tying up horses, and chambers that held kitchens and a five-year stock of provisions in case of siege.

The Crusaders were seriously short-handed at the end, with only 200 knights in a castle that could hold 2,000. They finally surrendered the castle in 1271 after a brief siege by a sizable Muslim army. Although the Crusaders had maintained a 200-year presence in the Holy Land, within 20 years of the fall of Krak des Chevaliers, they had withdrawn from the Holy Land completely.

Opposite: *The strategic castle overlooks the only gap in the coastal mountains between Turkey and Israel that allows passage from the sea to the interior of today's Syria. Crusaders took control of the ridge-top site in 1144, building fortifications according to the latest principles of military science.* Left: *Too solidly built to overpower, the castle was conquered by a trick: In 1271 the wily sultan Baybars sent a forged letter, ostensibly from the knights' commander in Tripoli, urging them to surrender. Weary and outnumbered, the knights were happy to accept Baybars's pledge of safe conduct to the sea.*

THE
Dome of the Rock

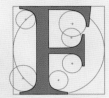 or Muslims, the Dome of the Rock ranks behind only Makkah and Medina as the world's holiest place. Sheltered beneath the dazzling golden dome—which was built according to perfect mathematical calculations—is the Holy Rock, whose associations touch three religions.

A shrine and place of pilgrimage, the Dome of the Rock rests upon the pedestal of the Temple Mount (or *Haram al-Sharif*), which occupies about 20 percent of Jerusalem's Old City. Traditionally, this

rock is believed to be where Abraham prepared to sacrifice his son as a sign of obedience to God. Solomon built a temple on the mount in 960 B.C. It is said this temple housed the Ark of the Covenant, the chest in which Moses placed the two stone tablets containing the Ten Commandments. Herod began rebuilding the temple in 20 B.C. And Muslims believe that it was from this same rock that the prophet Muhammad started on his ascent to heaven. (Today, guides point out his footprint in the Holy Rock.)

Left: *Among relics that draw pilgrims to the Dome of the Rock is a hair from Mohammad's head. Beneath the mosque, Muslims believe, the waters of Paradise flow and the spirits of the dead await Judgment Day. Opposite: The Dome of the Rock has an outer ambulatory with an octagonal arcade inside—a design suited to pilgrims rather than a congregation. The proud builder, Ibn Marwan, purportedly had 52 cleaners wash the mosque before prayers with a mixture of rose water, saffron, musk, and ambergris.*

The Dome of the Rock was built by Caliph Abd al-Malik ibn Marwan in the late seventh century. He intended the octagonal mosque to make it obvious that Islam was fully the equal of the religions that came before it: Judaism and Christianity. It is likely that he wanted the Dome of the Rock to outshine the city's Christian holy sites.

The mosque is certainly a wonder to behold, its exterior sheathed in marble slabs and polychrome glazed tiles that represent vines and flowers, geometric shapes, and inscriptions from the Koran. Inside, the walls are covered with bands of mother-of-pearl, green and gold glass, and mosaics. In the center rests the Holy Rock—which is, by comparison with its ornate surroundings, simple and basic, almost nondescript. Yet, according to tradition, it still retains the handprint of the archangel Gabriel, who held back the rock as it tried to follow the prophet Muhammad on his ascent to heaven.

Nearby is a reminder that this site is Judaism's most holy place, as well. A remnant of Herod's temple still stands and has come to be called the Western Wall, or sometimes the Wailing Wall. It remains a solemn destination for prayerful and devout Jews.

Petra

Jordan

Petra wasn't exactly a *lost* city. But by the early 1800s only the Bedouin herdsmen of the desert in what is now Jordan visited this ancient capital of the Nabataeans. To the world at large, its location was a mystery. The fabled city was said to lie concealed in a gorge somewhere between the Dead Sea and the Gulf of Aqaba—but maps were as hazy as the blowing sands.

Then in 1812 Swiss explorer Johann Ludwig Burckhardt disguised himself as "Ibrahim ibn Abd Allah," a bearded, turban-wearing, Arabic-speaking pilgrim. So convincing was his masquerade that no one stopped him from entering Petra, the "city in the rock," which no outsider had seen since the 12th century.

He found a city whose golden age had begun in the second century B.C., its prosperity stemming from expansive trade. Commerce brought cross-pollination from many other cultures and influenced Petra's architecture, which blended Arabic traditions with Hellenistic and Egyptian styles to create astonishing tombs, temples, and theaters—all carved into cliffs of Nubian sandstone.

In the first century A.D. Rome took control of Petra, and the Nabataeans' territory soon yielded much of the Empire's profits. Six centuries later earthquakes hit the city, and it was eventually abandoned.

As always, the city today is approached through a snaking mountain fissure, varying from 16 to 650 feet deep. After nearly a mile, the passage suddenly opens to reveal one of the world's most dramatic sights, *al-Khazneh*, the Treasury, thought to have been the tomb of a Nabataean king. Its façade—some 100 feet wide and 140 feet high—is embellished with soaring columns and statues of gods, mythological figures, and animals. Carved into the soft rock, the building takes on an otherworldly appearance when the sun strikes it, a rose glow that seems to come from within the rock itself.

The route into Petra next opens on a broad canyon where the Nabataeans built the bulk of their hidden city. The city includes a 7,000-seat theater, temples, and more royal tombs, all carved in rose-colored rock. Over everything hangs a hush, the silence of a lost world.

Opposite: *The tombs and temples of Petra, carved out of the cliffs themselves, appear suddenly when a traveler emerges from a three-quarter-mile-long passage through a red-rock mountain to encounter one of the most dramatic sights on Earth. In this dry terrain, the Nabataeans husbanded meager water supplies and used camels for desert transportation.*
Below: *Petra was both a bustling capital of the ancient Nabataeans and a place of burial monuments. Its structures were created 2,000 years ago, yet show an artistic sophistication that grew out of trade with distant cultures.*

THE
Pyramids of Giza and the Great Sphinx

Egypt

Of the Seven Wonders of the Ancient World, only one still exists—the pyramids of Giza. (Lists of the Seven Wonders vary, with some including all the pyramids and others only the Great Pyramid.) The Great Pyramid, Egypt's largest, is an astonishing structure completed more than 4,500 years ago.

How did the Egyptians, who built this pyramid around the 26th century B.C.,

Below: *The pyramids were not built by slaves, but by ordinary Egyptians working to pay off their taxes during idle time after the harvest was brought in. During their time of labor, the pharaoh gave them food and clothing.*
Opposite: *Stones of the ancients: When Herodotus saw the pyramids in 450* B.C., *they were already more distant in time from him than the birth of Jesus Christ is to us today.*

manage to quarry, transport, and raise into position some 2.3 million limestone blocks, each weighing at least 5,500 pounds? Archaeologists believe that perhaps 100,000 laborers used wooden sleds, papyrus ropes, and levers to drag the stones up ramps and into place. Then they fitted the blocks together without mortar.

Originally, the Great Pyramid had an outer casing of lustrous white limestone, long since stripped off and carted away as building material for the nearby city of Cairo. The smooth blocks were dressed so perfectly that even a knife blade couldn't be inserted between them. Upon completion, the pyramid rose to a height of more than 480 feet (now shorter by about 30 feet, since the top casing is gone).

Built as a tomb for Khufu (known to the Greeks as Cheops), the Great Pyramid stands near two others of descending size built by Khufu's son, Khafre (Chephren), and grandson, Menkure (Mykerinos). Khafre's pyramid, in the middle, actually appears to be the tallest, but this is an illusion created because it was built on higher ground— probably a deliberate move on Khafre's part in order to outdo his father.

All three pyramids date to the fourth Dynasty, and each was built as a tomb designed to protect the king's body and keep grave robbers from plundering the supplies the king would need in the next world. The pointed structure of each pyramid was also thought to serve as the departure point for the king's soul to ascend into the sky and join the sun god, Ra.

Of course, unknown grave robbers have come through the ages. A ninth-century caliph in search of treasure even blasted an opening on the north side, which has become the modern entrance. Today visitors entering the building follow a passage leading to the Great Gallery, a spacious corridor 28 feet high, and continue to the King's Chamber, whose walls are lined in solid red granite. The only thing tomb robbers left behind in the chamber was the king's broken sarcophagus—and that's only because it wouldn't fit through the entrance passage. Apparently it was put in position while the pyramid was still under construction.

What most archaeologists have considered ventilation shafts are now thought by a few to be "star shafts." One aims

The Great Sphinx

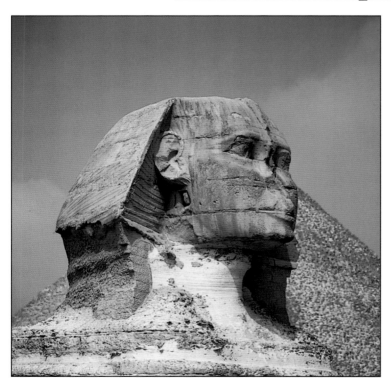

The three magnificent pyramids of Giza seem timeless, as if they dwell in a parallel world, solitary, abiding in their own mystery. But they have come down through the millennia with a companion—that enigmatic creature of stone, the Great Sphinx. This figure in repose is a lion with a man's face, probably that of Khafre. Carved entirely from a single outcrop of limestone bedrock, the Sphinx faces the rising sun.

Over the centuries the statue's stone has suffered damage from groundwater, eroding wind, and modern air pollution. It has also suffered indignity, such as having its nose shot off by 16th-century Turks who used the Sphinx for target practice.

More respectful, King Tuthmose IV believed the Sphinx spoke to him when he fell asleep in its shade. He dreamed that the figure asked him to clear away the encroaching desert sands that stifled it, and in reward Tuthmose IV was promised the throne of Egypt. When these events came to pass, to memorialize them the king erected a stone marker between the Sphinx's paws. Like the pyramids, the Sphinx presents the world with a mystery to confound the ages.

from the King's Chamber, for example, directly through the mass of the pyramid to frame the constellation of Orion's Belt (or rather, the spot where the constellation would have been located in the ancient sky). Not only were Orion's stars linked with the god Osiris, but their appearance in the sky occurred at the same time as the Nile's annual life-giving flood, so Orion was of great significance.

The complex of the slightly smaller Khafre pyramid is the most complete of all, with a causeway leading from the Valley Temple, where the king's body was mummified. Priests brought the body up the 440-yard-long causeway to its burial place in the pyramid. The pyramid still retains some of its original limestone casing at the top, offering a hint of its once radiant glory. In contrast, the smaller Pyramid of Menkure has courses of red granite blocks around its base, a casing that was never completed.

The pyramids stand amidst a complex of structures built by ancient Egyptians for funerary procedures and other purposes. The dry desert climate has helped to preserve many ruins.

THE
Temple at Karnak

Egypt

Imagine yourself awakening in ancient Egypt. You walk to the temple complex at Karnak along a processional way lined with ram-headed sphinxes. Soon you enter a hall that is a forest of stone, with 134 columns—each one so huge that it takes six people with their arms stretched wide to encircle it. The immensity of this hypostyle hall is such that it eclipses Paris's Notre Dame Cathedral.

Taking its scale from the gods themselves, the Karnak temple complex was devoted to the Theban Triad: Amun, Mut, and their son Khonsu. Founded during Egypt's Middle Kingdom, roughly 2000–1800 B.C., the 53-acre temple compound was developed by successive Egyptian kings over a period of 1,700 years.

In the Temple of Amun rises Egypt's tallest obelisk, which memorializes Thutmose I's daughter, Hatshepsut. Fashioned of rose granite, the obelisk stands more than 90 feet tall and weighs 340 tons. Hatshepsut—history's only female pharaoh—had the obelisk inscribed with a greeting to the ages that begins: "O ye people who see this monument in years to come and speak of that which I have made…" The stone pillar today is well preserved and graffiti free because of Hatshepsut's vengeful nephew, Thutmose III.

Left: *A row of enigmatic, ram-headed sphinxes, carved of stone, are just a few of the ancient wonders on view at the remarkable Temple of Karnak.* Above: *Despite their massive construction, the temple's buildings are carved delicately. In spots they still show the brightly painted designs that once enlivened the vast complex.*

In trying to wipe out every trace of his aunt at Karnak, he had a wall built in front of the obelisk to hide it. Instead, the wall ended up protecting the obelisk down through the centuries.

In another precinct loom two colossal figures of Amun and Amunet. Not coincidentally, the faces bear a resemblance to the king who had them erected, Tutankhamen, who ascended the throne in

One of Egypt's greatest sights, the Temple at Karnak is unsurpassed among ancient religious monuments in its quality and complexity. The colossus of Pinudjem greets visitors at the western entrance.

1361 B.C. The Karnak complex also includes a sanctuary decorated by Alexander the Great, not to mention a courtyard where archaeologists unearthed an astounding cache of 17,000 bronze statues from the Temple of Amun.

Karnak even has a Sacred Lake, its waters once used by the temple priests for ritual cleansing. On one shore stands a large granite scarab—a symbol of Amun, the sun god, at his rebirth each morning after his journey through night. At Karnak, the gods of ancient Egypt still live.

Abu Simbel

Egypt

Egypt's greatest egotist and builder, Ramses II erected more temples and statues— of himself, naturally—than any other pharaoh. His self-glorification campaign worked well, because more than 3,200 years after his death, we still remember him as Ramses the Great.

His most impressive works are the two rock temples at Abu Simbel. Carved into a mountain on the west bank of the Nile, the Great Temple of Ramses II is guarded by four commanding statues of the pharaoh. Ramses wanted to impress the rebellious Nubians with his mighty power, so the statues tower 65 feet tall— and that's sitting down. Each figure weighs some 1,200 tons. The statues surely induced awe in friend and foe alike.

Within the temple is a hypostyle hall, whose roof rests on eight columns fronted with figures of, not surprisingly, Ramses. Deeper inside, the sacred sanctuary is adorned with statues of four gods: Re-Horakhty, Amun, Ptah, and Ramses' deified self. The pharaoh's engineers oriented the temple so perfectly that each year on February 22 and October 22 (not coincidentally Ramses' birthday and the anniversary of his coronation), the light of the rising sun streams through the temple entrance, travels 200 feet, and, like heav-

enly fire, sets the figure of Ramses aglow.

In the 1960s Abu Simbel's temples were imperiled by the building of Aswan High Dam and the rising waters of Lake Nasser that resulted from it. In an incredible feat of modern engineering, the temples were cut from the rock cliff, carved up into hundreds of massive blocks (estimates range from 950 to 2,000), some weighing as much as 33 tons, and moved to a higher location nearby. Ramses' temple was carefully positioned on the new site so the rising sun still penetrates the sanctuary twice a year.

The pink sandstone Temple of Hathor, the cow-headed goddess of love, was built to honor Ramses' favorite wife, Queen Nefertari. Her temple is, of course, smaller than Ramses',

and many of the huge statues adorning it represent the mighty, towering pharaoh. Ramses the Great made sure that his legacy would be larger than life.

Opposite: *Four figures of the great Ramses II weigh 2.4 million pounds apiece. In 27 B.C. one statue lost its top half in an earthquake. The great king—as monumental a personality in life as in death—took dozens of wives and had 178 children before he died at age 97.* Below: *Standing within the interior of the temple are figures that were formerly painted, like their surroundings, and lavishly gilded. Remarkably, the entire complex was moved during the 1960s to make way for the creation of Lake Nasser.*

THE
Kaaba and Al-Haram Mosque

Saudi Arabia

To Muslims around the world, the most sacred spot on earth is a black-draped, square shrine called the Kaaba, which stands in the central courtyard of the vast Al-Haram Mosque in Makkah. It is toward this spot that Muslims turn five times a day in prayer. And it is the goal of every devout Muslim to make a pilgrimage to the Kaaba at least once in a lifetime.

Islamic tradition asserts that Abraham and Ishmael built the Kaaba as a copy of God's house in heaven. Cube shaped, it is 50 feet high and made of gray stone and marble. Its early history is unclear, but it is known that when Muhammad conquered Makkah in 630, he destroyed pagan idols inside. Since then, Muslims have focused their devotion on the Kaaba. The inside is empty, except for three pillars that hold up the roof and some hanging lamps of silver and gold.

On arrival, the pilgrim must walk around the Kaaba seven times, asking forgiveness and, if possible, touching and kissing the Black Stone mounted on one of the Kaaba's walls. According to Islamic belief, Adam was given this stone after he was expelled from Paradise, so he could obtain pardon for his sins. The stone was initially white, it is said, but by absorbing the sins of millions of pilgrims, it has turned black. Now cracked into pieces, the Black Stone is protected with a silver frame. Some observers declare that the object is a meteorite, but the devout consider it a stone from heaven.

Makkah's population increases by a million people when Muslims make their hajj to the city during the holy month of pilgrimage. To accommodate the flood of humanity, the Al-Haram Mosque is regularly enlarged and now contains 1.7 million square feet of space. It can hold 300,000 people at one time. As they throng the mosque and circumambulate the Kaaba, people are jammed chest to chest, even in the late hours of night. But their spirits are lifted high.

Left: *As many as 300,000 Muslims can fit into the mosque, where they surround the simple cube-shaped Kaaba, the holiest shrine of Islam. Most of the year the cube is draped in a huge cloth of black brocade, the* kiswah. *Opposite: Only Muslims may enter Makkah, whose holy mosque is enlarged regularly to accommodate the thronging pilgrims. During its history, the Kaaba has been destroyed and rebuilt several times.*

THE
Forbidden City

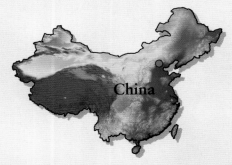

China

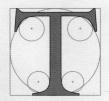here's no false advertising here. Beijing's Forbidden City was exactly what it claimed to be. This maze of 800 buildings was off limits to ordinary mortals, being the exclusive precinct of China's emperors and their courts for 500 years. Regular Chinese were prohibited from even coming near the walls. This complex has sometimes been called the "place with 9,999 and a half rooms" (because only the palace of heaven could have a perfect 10,000 rooms), but in reality it has about 8,700 rooms and halls.

Begun in the early 15th century by the Yongle emperor, who put 200,000 laborers to work on the project, the Forbidden City was the home of 24 successive Ming and Qing emperors through 1924. Protected within a moat and 30-foot-

high walls, the "Sons of Heaven" were elevated above earthly matters, a fact reflected in the very architecture of the palace. Ceremonial halls are perched on a marble plinth several feet above the surrounding courtyard.

Beautifully planned, the architecture of the Forbidden City maintains a harmonious sense of poise between buildings and open space. The complex is symmetrically balanced along a north-south axis, but the design is never rigid or monotonous.

The vast outer courtyard, also known as the "Sea of Flagstones," had room for imperial audiences of 100,000 people. Like an ocean, it washes around

The Hall of Supreme Harmony, the first hall visitors encounter when entering the Forbidden City from the south, is the largest wooden structure in China.

three great halls that make up the ceremonial heart of the Forbidden City. The largest, the Hall of Supreme Harmony, was reserved for august occasions such as coronations or the emperor's birthday celebration. Only the ruler himself could use the marble entry ramp adorned with carved dragons. In the hall, amidst clanging gongs and clouds of incense, prostrate courtiers were required to strike the floor nine times with their foreheads. No doubt the emperor made a stunning impression.

The hall displays treasures such as jade musical chimes and the splendidly ornamented Dragon Throne, from which the emperor issued his absolute decisions.

No group of historic buildings in China is larger or better preserved than the Forbidden City, the 180-acre Imperial Palace complex, home to the emperors for five centuries.

Outside the hall a bronze turtle, symbolizing long life, puffs incense smoke from its mouth. On the roof, ornamental dragons—

Lions are considered excellent guardians and can often be found in China protecting entrances of various kinds from evil spirits. This lion of gilded bronze, along with its partner, stands alert before its assigned gate. Seven pairs of lions protect seven gates in the Forbidden City.

standing 11 feet tall and weighing 4.5 tons—are believed to protect the building from fire because they draw clouds and rain.

The ruler used the nearby Hall of Middle Harmony as a dressing room before important ceremonies. He also greeted important foreigners here and addressed the royal progeny, children born to his wives and many concubines.

In the Hall of Preserving Harmony, candidates took examinations for the world's first civil-service bureaucracy. Inside stands a huge chunk of marble carved with motifs of dragons and clouds.

Weighing 250 tons, it was transported to Beijing on a pathway of ice created by sluicing water onto the winter roads.

Beyond these outer precincts lies the Forbidden City's inner courtyard, whose three palaces served the Ming and Qing Dynasties as imperial residences. The Palace of Heavenly Purity, the emperor's sleeping quarters, is guarded by incense burners shaped like cranes and tortoises. Emperors and empresses consummated their marriages in the Palace of Earthly Tranquility, whose small wedding chamber is painted completely red. The room was last used in 1922, after the wedding of the Manchu child emperor Pu-yi, who compared the gaudy décor to "a melted red wax candle."

Uncomfortable there, Pu-yi abandoned his wedding chamber for the more familiar Hall of Mental Cultivation. In its apartments emperors spent most of their time, living and working. During the

1800s, the Dowager Empress Cixi received visitors here from behind a screen, as foreigners and Chinese of lower station were not allowed to lay eyes on so lofty a personage.

In many ways the emperor and his court lived in a gilded prison. They rarely dared to venture beyond the Forbidden City's walls, and then only with elaborate precautions. The emperor rode in a palanquin, a closed and covered reclining couch carried by four servants. Military guards, the secret service scouting the route, and a policy of never revealing which palanquin carried the emperor were just some of the stratagems used to safeguard the ruler outside the Imperial Palace.

One of the few places the people closed inside the complex could relax was the Imperial Garden. Wandering among the pavilions and ponds, pines, flowers, and bamboo—all the classical sights of Chinese gardening—residents had an all-too-rare experience of nature, the kind of simple pleasure that commoners enjoyed every day. But that was in the world outside, beyond the high walls of the Forbidden City.

This inviting doorway beckons visitors to enter the lavish luxury within. The studs on each door are arranged in nine rows of nine. Nine was the royal number, and only the emperor was allowed this design.

THE
Terra-cotta Army

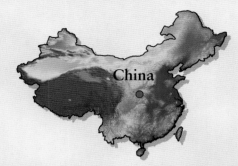

China

Ranked in battle formation, many thousands of life-size terra-cotta soldiers and their horses protect the tomb of Emperor Qin Shi Huang. Although strikingly beautiful, the army was never meant to be seen by mortal eyes. The clay figures were buried more than 2,000 years ago in underground vaults, ready to escort the emperor into eternal life.

The splendid treasure, the legacy of the first emperor of a unified China, was discovered in 1974 by peasants digging a well. Among the terra-cotta warriors so far uncovered in three vaults are archers, cavalry, charioteers, and armored soldiers wielding spears and dagger-axes. The soldiers' military ranks can be determined by examining their hairstyles and the fine points of their uniforms. (Originally, their clothes were painted green, red, purple, and blue, but only a few traces of pigment remain.)

Remarkably, every figure has unique facial features and may actually be a portrait of an individual imperial guard. Yet the statues were in a sense generic; the mostly hollow figures were mass produced, then the individually modeled heads and hands were put on.

Like real soldiers, the terra-cotta warriors originally carried actual cross-

bows, swords, and spears. Some 10,000 weapons already have been found in the vaults. Because the swords' metal surfaces were specially treated, they defied corrosion so effectively that the blades still remain sharp, even after 2,000 years in the ground. Somewhat ominously, arrowheads found here were made of a poisonous alloy of lead—just like the arrows that were set up as traps in the emperor's tomb itself.

In one vault a great number of clay warriors were found shattered and broken, the aftermath of their centuries-long vigil beneath the ground. Uncovered now, they create the impression of a battlefield of fallen soldiers—a reminder, perhaps, of the futility of war and the vanity of emperors.

Opposite: *In the largest vault, about 1,000 figures have been uncovered so far, perhaps only one-eighth of the total number of warriors buried here.* Below: *Great care was evidently taken by the artisans to ensure that each warrior is a distinct individual. Models may have been employed during the process. If that is so, their likenesses have survived long after their identities have been lost.*

THE
Great Wall of China

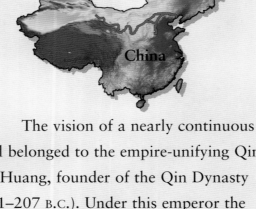

China

Rippling across the landscape of northern China like a brown-scaled dragon, the Great Wall stretches from the desert to the sea. And like a dragon, the wall has a mythical aura and an important place in Asian culture—and in the world.

Archaeologists disagree on when the earliest parts of the wall were built, but it may have been as early as the seventh century B.C. What is clear is that work was begun to connect the various fortifying walls during the third century B.C. This work went on into the 17th century and produced a structure that extended about 4,000 miles across China.

The vision of a nearly continuous wall belonged to the empire-unifying Qin Shi Huang, founder of the Qin Dynasty (221–207 B.C.). Under this emperor the Great Wall took on its present immense character. Older defensive walls separating once-rival territories were linked together to form a continuous earthen barrier against barbarian invaders from the north.

Later emperors lengthened the wall, but rulers of the medieval Ming Dynasty made it their primary enterprise, facing the wall with stone and brick and adding inno-

vations. Near mountain passes of particularly strategic value, they erected as many as 20 parallel walls to confound attackers.

In the end the Great Wall attained a colossal scale. It averaged 22 feet thick, with enough room on top for five horse soldiers to ride side by side. The wall also served as an elevated highway for soldiers and traders. In addition, guards in the beacon towers could send signals—using drums, smoke from smoldering wolf dung, or cannon blasts—all the way down the line to the emperor in Beijing.

Paradoxically, the wall wasn't a fully effective line of defense. Various invaders managed to breach the barrier. Every sentry was a potential weak spot, because sentries could be bribed. In the mid-1600s at a well-fortified mountain pass near the Yellow Sea, a turncoat general simply let Manchu horse soldiers ride through. The invaders marched into Beijing, established a new dynasty, and did no further work on the Great Wall—which had, after all, failed to hinder their invasion. During the next three centuries, much of the wall crumbled or was overgrown.

Today many sections of the Great Wall have been reconstructed to meet the arrival of a new force of modern invaders—some 10,000 tourists every day.

Left: *Construction of the wall began more than 2,000 years ago and cost many thousands of lives. People today view the Great Wall as a world wonder of great beauty, but it was actually a symbol of oppression, similar to the modern Berlin Wall. Opposite: The Great Wall is the only historical feature that cartographers mark on world maps. It has often been said that astronauts could see the wall from the moon, but NASA insists this is not true. Never wholly effective as a deterrent to invaders, the Great Wall enjoys its greatest success as a modern tourist attraction.*

Potala Palace

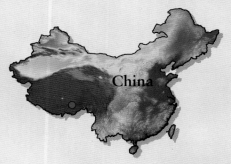

China

Welcome to the land of what once was. Here in Tibet, the Potala Palace was long the home of the Dalai Lama, a thriving monastery, and the hub of government administration. Although monks still maintain the shrines, under China's domination of Tibet the palace has become a museum, a repository of things past.

Yet the Potala Palace remains a wonder of architecture, requiring the skills of 1,500 artists and skilled workers and 7,000 laborers. The exotic structure stands 13 stories high and contains more than 1,000 rooms. Located in Lhasa at 12,000 feet above sea level, the palace is surrounded by transcendent mountains, lakes, and snows that must have helped generate the Tibetans' highly spiritual culture.

Tibet's beliefs developed around the seventh century, when Buddhism arrived and blended with local animistic doctrines. Today religious pilgrims from all over Tibet come to the Potala Palace, thronging its chapels, admiring its gold and bejeweled treasures, making offerings of yak butter, and prostrating themselves.

The palace is divided into two sections. The White Palace, built in the mid-17th century, provided living quarters for the fifth through the fourteenth Dalai Lamas. The latter's apartment remains just as it was in 1959, when he and some 80,000 followers left Tibet and took flight across the Himalayas to India to escape the invading Chinese.

From the White Palace, pilgrims climb to the central Red Palace, completed four decades later and packed with chapels, ornate statues, and the gem-embellished tombs of past Dalai Lamas. The fifth Dalai Lama's tomb, made from two *tons* of gold, stands three stories tall.

Tibet's most venerated image, a solid gold statue of Sakyamuni, is housed not far away in Jokhang Temple, the country's holiest shrine. At the 1,350-year-old temple, monks chant, incense burners waft juniper smoke up toward heaven, and it seems that the world of long ago and far away is still very much with us.

Left: *Potala Palace was built in the 17th century on the site of a vanished palace of a thousand years earlier. Home of ten successive Dalai Lamas, it is the burial place of all but one.* Opposite: *On top of* Marpo Ri, *or Red Mountain, stands Potala Palace, the great landmark of Lhasa. Before the Dalai Lama left in 1959, the palace served not only as the leader's home and seat of government, but also as a monastery and fortress.*

THE
Taj Mahal

India

Arguably the most perfect building on Earth, the Taj Mahal is an Indian ruler's timeless memorial to his lost, lamented love. This white marble pearl of architecture was once described by poet Rabindranath Tagore as "a teardrop on the cheek of eternity." Like love and tears, it cannot be captured in mere words.

The perfectly symmetrical Taj—a central dome surrounded by four smaller domes, with minarets at each corner, all reflected in a long pool—appears exceptionally lovely at dawn and sunset, when the luminescent marble building seems almost to float on air. Its beauty changes throughout the day. Sometimes the Taj Mahal is veiled in mist, at other times glowing soft pink, or shadowed in pearl gray, or softening to creamy yellow, or gleaming white under the blazing sun of Agra. The changing illumination is actually

a decorative motif, designed to produce an assortment of responses in the viewer. And according to the principles of Mogul architecture, light symbolizes the presence of Allah.

Completed in 1653, the Taj Mahal was erected by the Mogul ruler Shah Jahan to honor the memory and enshrine the

body of his favorite wife, Mumtaz Mahal ("Elect of the Palace"), who died while giving birth to their 14th child. Building the mausoleum took 22 years and 20,000 workers. A convoy of 1,000 elephants hauled the marble blocks, each weighing more than two tons, from quarries more than 200 miles away.

The massive scale and grandeur of the Taj Mahal is counterpoised by the extreme delicacy of its ornamentation. Particularly elegant adornments are the floral inlays of precious stones brought from various locales: lapis lazuli from Sri Lanka,

Opposite: The centuries-old Taj Mahal is menaced by Agra's all-too-modern air pollution. Factory emissions mix with moisture in the air to create sulphuric acid, which eats into the surface of the tomb, yellows the pure white marble, and causes it to flake. Right: The Mogul design principle of symmetry is reflected in the monument's arches, towers, inlays, and other features, ensuring that the Taj Mahal delights the eye when viewed from virtually any angle or distance.

turquoise from Tibet, mother of pearl from the Indian Ocean, carnelian from Iraq, crystal and green jade from Turkistan.

Like a treasure, the Taj Mahal is protected behind a towering gateway of red sandstone that looms 100 feet high. Next comes a garden laid out in typical Mogul style, with symmetry as the guiding rule. Waterways divide the garden into quarters to symbolize the Islamic Gardens of Paradise, whose four rivers run with water, milk, wine, and honey. In the garden's former days of glory, bright fish filled the waterways, colorful birds flitted through the air, and symmetrically planted trees symbolized death (cypresses) and life (fruit trees).

The tomb is flanked by a mosque of red sandstone that consecrates the grounds and by an identical replica called the *Jawab* ("answer"), whose doorway faces away from Makkah, making the building unusable for prayer. At the tomb's four corners stand minarets that slant outward ever so slightly—a precaution in case of earthquake, designed to insure that the tall, slender towers fall away from the tomb rather than collapse onto it.

True to Mogul principles of architectural symmetry, the tomb itself takes the shape of a square, measuring 186 feet on each side. Its central arch is set off on either side by smaller arches. The width of the marble pedestal on which the tomb stands equals the tomb's height. And the height of the dome is equal to the height of the façade below.

The globular dome resembles a pearl, recalling Muhammad's portrayal of the throne of God as a dome of white pearl resting upon four pillars. Using an architectural innovation developed in Central Asia, the dome is actually of double construction, a design that allows more height.

The tomb's octagonal main chamber holds the memorial to Mumtaz Mahal, set behind a delicately cut marble screen that transmits an illumination as ethereal as lace. Shah Jahan's memorial is beside it. The inlay of precious stones is so elaborate on these monuments that a single leaf or flower may be fashioned of up to 60 or 70 separate pieces. The actual tombs of the royal duo lie directly below, in the crypt.

When Shah Jahan built this undying monument to romantic love, Mughal power was on the wane, and the project consumed much of the empire's wealth. Furthermore, the inconsolable ruler was quite distracted from matters of state. Eventually his son, Aurangzeb, staged a coup and seized power. Strict and devout, the son imprisoned the father in the nearby fort at Agra. The despondent Shah Jahan spent his last years gazing across at his wife's memorial of pure white marble, the magnificent Taj Mahal.

Exquisitely fashioned, right down to its illusionistic stone paving, the Taj Mahal was Shah Jahan's perfect monument to his wife of 19 years, Mumtaz Mahal. She traveled with his army, advised him on state business, and then in 1631 died in childbirth, leaving the Mogul ruler stricken with grief.

Ellora Caves

 arved into the volcanic cliffs at Ellora, this series of 34 cave shrines transform Buddhist, Hindu, and Jain beliefs into three dimensions. The sculptured designs are highly elaborate and even include freestanding structures. (For comparison, try to imagine a European church carved from solid stone.)

The work was done in three stages, starting with 12 Buddhist caves created between A.D. 600 and 900. Most are monastery halls, called *viharas*, where monks once meditated, worshiped, and studied. The halls contain statues of the Buddha, often flanked by guardian figures such as the two *bodhisattvas* Padmapani (the lotus bearer, symbolizing purity) and Vajrapani (holding the thunderbolt of esoteric knowledge).

Another 17 Hindu caves from A.D. 650 to 1000 are packed with dynamic carved scenes focusing on Shiva, god of destruction. The famous Kailash Temple is a colossal model of Shiva's home on a peak

of the Tibetan plateau. It was carved from the cliff itself, starting from the top and working downward through solid rock. The temple measures 165 feet long and 96 feet high, an astonishing achievement for craftsmen this long ago.

The carved stone entry screen signifies the threshold between two worlds, the profane and the sacred. Within is a shrine for Nandi, the bull that is Shiva's vehicle, an assembly hall, and a sanctuary topped with

a squat pyramidal tower. Everywhere are carved images of river goddesses, sages, and gods such as the elephant-headed Ganesh, bringer of good fortune, and the bowman Kama, god of desire, whose five arrows represent the senses. For worshipers through the centuries who have been unable to read, carved mythological scenes take the place of religious texts in offering instruction.

The last five caves (A.D. 800–1000) are dedicated to Jainism, one of the world's oldest religions. These caves, not nearly as spectacular as the Hindu caves, are carved with simple Jain images such as the potbellied Mahavir, lions and elephants, and a ceiling that resembles a huge lotus.

And so, in a single location, the Ellora Caves offer a course in comparative religion and Asian art.

Left: *Elaborately detailed images make the 17 Hindu caves positively vibrate with life. The artwork focuses on the god Shiva and his vehicle, the bull Nandi.* Opposite: *The temples were carved out of 100,000 cubic yards of rock. Stone provided an ideal building material in a place regularly hit by monsoon rains, because it endures much longer than wood.*

Shwedagon Pagoda

Burma

"A golden mystery...a beautiful winking wonder" is what Rudyard Kipling called this Buddhist shrine topped with 5,448 diamonds and 2,317 rubies, sapphires, and other precious gems. Domed like a bell, the Buddhist shrine, or stupa, is literally gold plated, using 8,688 sheets of the precious yellow metal.

Burma's most sacred Buddhist site has a mystical aura that attracts some 10,000 pilgrims annually. Shwedagon Pagoda, it is said, houses eight hairs from the head of the Buddha. When these were installed in their chamber, remarkable things reportedly happened: "Rays emitted by the Hairs penetrated up to the heavens above and down to hell...the earth quaked...the winds of the ocean blew...lightning flashed...gems rained down until they were knee deep...all trees of the Himalayas, though not in season, bore blossoms and fruit."

Begun in the fifth century B.C., Shwedagon Pagoda has been rebuilt and enlarged over

Opposite: The pagoda is radiant with light gleaming from 60 tons of gold pounded into thin leaves. On the summit rises a pennant-shaped vane topped with a 76-carat diamond orb. Left: "All about, shrines and pagodas were jumbled pell-mell with the confusion with which trees grow in the jungle," wrote Somerset Maugham. "Their gold and marble faintly gleaming, they had a fantastic richness." Above: The pagoda is devoted to the Buddha and contains eight venerated hairs from his head, reportedly given to two Burmese traders in India by the Buddha himself.

the centuries, with treasure added regularly. Bells of pure gold and silver (1,485 of them) hang on the *hti*, or umbrella portion of the stupa.

After a queen donated her weight in gold, her successor raised the ante to four times his weight, and these gifts were beaten into gold leaf to apply to the stupa. On each of the eight sides of the base stand eight smaller stupas, for a total of 64 swirling about the golden shrine. No wonder Aldous Huxley observed that the pagoda has a "merry-go-round style of architecture." He also said that it serves the throng of pilgrims as "a sort of sacred fun fair."

Four stairways lead to the stupa's upper terrace. After seeing the sight, Somerset Maugham said of the Shwedagon Pagoda that it was "glistening with gold, like a sudden hope in the dark night of the soul."

Angkor Wat

Cambodia

A French naturalist named Henri Mouhot in 1860 stumbled across a city of stone hidden in the tangled forest of Cambodia. It had been built long ago, the locals told him, by a vanished race of giant gods. "Grander than anything left by Greece or Rome," Mouhot said about the lost city of Angkor, with its more than 100 temples and remarkable carvings.

This work was begun in 802 not by giant gods but by Jayavarman II, a Khmer king who chose to build his capital here. (*Angkor* means "city" in the Khmer lan-

Vishnu, the Hindu god of preservation, greets visitors to the temple at both the east and west entrances. Angkor Wat's builder, Suryavarman II, constructed the temple in dedication to the deity.

guage.) Within two centuries perhaps a million people lived here. The city stretched across the plain for 100 square miles.

The finest temple here, and probably the largest religious monument ever built, is the 500-acre Angkor Wat. Built in the early 12th century by Suryavarman II, it is considered the peak of classical Khmer architecture and art. It is dedicated to the Hindu god Vishnu, the preserver—as well as to his human embodiment in Suryavarman II, who was considered a god-king.

Angkor Wat consists of rectangular enclosures that frame a "temple mountain" designed with an allegorical meaning. The high central sanctuary symbolically corresponds to Mount Meru, the sacred mountain where Hindu gods dwell at the center of the universe. Meru's five peaks are represented by the temple's five towers. The surrounding walls stand for mountains at the fringe of the world, and the moat is the ocean farther out. The central towers are reachable by twelve stairways that suggest the steep slopes of Mount Meru.

The towers are designed to look like sprouting lotus buds, and at one time they may have been covered in gold. Throughout the temple complex, carvings and sculptures depict gods, battle scenes, dancers, events in Hindu mythology, and other images. Working in sandstone, a fairly soft material, made the construction project easier for the 5,000 artisans and 50,000 laborers who built the temple over a period of some three decades.

Creating a mystic link with the eternal movement of the heavens that revolve around the temple, the buildings and statues of Angkor Wat line up with the solar equinoxes and solstices.

The walls of the outer gallery are covered in bas-relief carvings that reach more than six feet high and are said to be the longest continuous bas-reliefs in the world. The carved scenes tell stories from Hindu religious epics—the *Ramayana* and the *Mahabharata*—and narrate Vishnu's adventures. Supposedly, the bevies of *apsaras,* or heavenly dancers, who adorn the temple were carved using the king's own bare-breasted harem as models. The women's exotic hairstyles and jeweled collars illustrate high fashion as it was practiced in the area eight centuries ago.

Angkor Wat and the surrounding city thrived until 1431, when invaders

from Siam (current-day Thailand) arrived. Badly damaged, Angkor was soon abandoned. But the forest itself proved an even more destructive invader. Vines, creepers, and rampant fig trees strangled the buildings and pushed masonry walls asunder, swallowing up the forgotten city.

Fortunately, Angkor Wat fared better than many other structures, because Buddhist monks arrived with the Siamese invaders and occupied the temple. In the

high central tower, once the sacred precincts of the Hindu god Siva, the monks placed a huge figure of Buddha.

After Angkor's rediscovery in the mid-1800s, French and Cambodian archaeologists restored many ruins. But their work was undone in the 1970s, when Angkor was infiltrated by Khmer Rouge guerrillas who looted temples, decapitated sculptures, and sold the spoils on the black market to raise cash for war. In the early

The 12th-century temple was erected around the same time as the Cathedral of Notre Dame in Paris, and it occupies about the same acreage as the Forbidden City in Beijing.

1990s, thieves ran wild through the temples, cutting the heads off the famous *apsaras* and causing extensive damage. Illicit art dealers acquired many of the treasures from Angkor, and quite a few sculptures later reemerged in western auction houses and private collections.

THE
Golden Pavilion

Japan

This graceful pavilion is probably the most recognizable temple in Japan—and no wonder. How many buildings are entirely covered in gold? Shining in the soft light, the Golden Pavilion, or *Kinkakuji*, as it is known in Japanese, looks like a glittering jewel box. And the beauty of the temple—with its two upswept roofs reflected in a tranquil pond—once brought it tragedy.

In 1950 a disturbed Buddhist temple novice burned the 14th-century pavilion to its foundations. Seduced by its beauty, and apparently unable to control his covetousness, he torched the building. Within five years, however, the Golden Pavilion rose again. On the new roof, appropriately, perches a phoenix.

The pavilion was built as a retirement villa for the shogun Ashikaga Yoshimitsu, who, after withdrawing from public life, exercised power in the background by installing his ten-year-old son as shogun. Interested in the artistic life, he collected Sung Chinese artwork, staged traditional No plays, and practiced Zen and the tea ceremony. He also played host at boating parties on the pavilion's pond. When he died, his retirement villa was converted into a temple, in accordance with his wishes.

The much-admired pavilion rises in three stories, each having a different architectural style and reflecting a different aspect of the shogun who built it. The first floor is a residential palace, complete with a covered dock for the shogun's pleasure boat; the second is a Buddhist prayer hall or samurai house; and the third is a small Zen temple with sliding doors and bell-shaped windows.

Set on pillars, the Golden Pavilion extends over the pond, a popular design of the Shinden style during the Heian period of Japanese history. A person approaching sees two pavilions, as the water reflects the image. On the exterior of the graceful building, a layer of shimmering gold leaf creates an unforgettable picture.

Left: *The three stories of this architectural crossbreed reflect different aspects of the shogun who built the 14th-century original: palace residence, samurai hall, Zen temple.* Opposite: *The Golden Pavilion is reflected in a tranquil pond—a planned effect, so that the reflection produces a second pavilion. The temple's setting on the pond also implies its suspension between Earth and heaven.*

THE
Great Buddha

Japan

A powerful tsunami swept ashore at Kamakura, Japan, in 1495, knocking the city flat and ripping away the wooden temple that housed the Great Buddha, the *Daibutsu*, a colossal bronze statue that had been sitting there in peaceful repose for two-and-a-half centuries. When the tidal wave passed, the figure was still sitting serenely.

The Great Buddha has stayed out in the elements for another five centuries, and today it sits there still—nearly 40 feet high, even without the pedestal—meditating and showing a compassionate visage to the world.

Cast in 1252 by sculptors Ono Goroemon and Tanji Hisatomo, the statue represents Amida, the Buddha of the Western Paradise, who by nature is merciful to all people, regardless of their sta-

The 1495 tidal wave that destroyed the Buddha's sheltering temple is not the only natural disaster to have struck here. An earthquake measuring 8.3 struck Japan in 1923 and, although it damaged the statue's base, did not apparently disturb the serenely meditating Great Buddha.

tion in life. To prevent the very tall statue from appearing remote or distant to a

viewer below, the figure was purposely cast with its features out of proportion. The head and shoulders are actually too massive for the lower body. Because of this, when viewed from a distance the statue may look unbalanced, with too much weight at the top. But a person standing just in front of the Great Buddha, as the sculptor intended, sees everything in proper proportion.

To discover how the 90-ton statue was constructed, visitors can go inside the hollow figure via stairs that reach to the shoulders. Seams joining the statue's separately cast layers are revealed, along with 750 years' worth of scratches, cracks, and scars in the bronze.

The Great Buddha's long earlobes have been described as hanging "like dried fruit on a tropical tree." Some of the figure's other facial features are also customary artistic devices, such as its 656 curls of hair. Overall, the masterful design, combined with the patina of age derived from facing the weather for more than 500 years, has created a figure that never fails to capture people and place them under its tranquil aura.

Seated on the grounds of Kotoku Temple, the Great Buddha measures nearly 40 feet high and 30 feet from knee to knee. Because the sculptor carefully misbalanced the upper and lower parts of the statue, the Buddha appears top-heavy from a distance but perfectly proportioned when viewed up close.

Borobudur

Indonesia

Building Borobudur—the world's largest stupa, or Buddhist shrine—required several thousand workers and the better part of a century. For its construction, peasant laborers assembled a casing of unmortared stone over a hillock in central Java, Indonesia. This feat required them to hew and transport between one and two million stones without modern engineering techniques or tools—only ropes, hammers, rolling logs, and muscle power.

Even more incredible than its scale is the fineness of Borobudur's carvings, which have been called "a magnificent Buddhist rosary in stone." The carvings are mounted along an ascending three-mile path that represents the journey of the human spirit along the road to spiritual perfection.

At the base, a series of bas-reliefs depict the transitory Sphere of Desire, with its earthly pleasures and punishments. This base has now become nearly covered by earth and stone. Moving higher on the processional path and five square levels, the pilgrim encounters a more spiritually elevated world, the Sphere of Form, with carved scenes from the life of Prince Siddhartha as he progresses toward enlightenment as Gautama Buddha.

The more than 1,200 bas-relief panels in the five levels also depict scenes of life in Indonesia more than a thousand years ago, vibrant with farmers

The temple was abandoned soon after it was built, then it slowly deteriorated in Java's wet climate. Restoration completed in 1984 took ten years and $25 million, but it saved the great monument from likely ruin.

and warriors, musicians and dancing girls, ships and elephants and kings. More than 400 carved Buddhas appear along the path as well.

The next levels are three circular terraces representing the Sphere of Formlessness, where 72 latticed stupas hold statues of the Buddha. Reaching through the open mesh to touch one of the figures is thought to bring good luck. The pilgrim's final steps upward, as he ascends from the material world to the sublime, reach a large central stupa. This summit represents release into nirvana, an ineffable state of wisdom and compassion. Now the pilgrim has reached the center of the universe, or the center of the self—or perhaps they are the same thing.

Seen from above, Borobudur resembles a mandala, or spiritual diagram of the universe. The stupa's lower square platforms correspond to the earthly plane, while the upper round platforms represent the circular vault of the heavens—thus, the stupa symbolizes the divine union between the two worlds.

Sydney Opera House

Australia

Like a flotilla of grand ships under sail, gliding across one of the world's great natural harbors, the Sydney Opera House arrests every visitor's attention. Since opening in 1973, this performance complex has become the very emblem of Sydney, while also raising the cultural tone of a city that began as a convict settlement and has retained a raucous edge of honky-tonk.

Each year the Opera House presents some 3,000 performances in its main spaces—the 1,547-seat Opera Theatre (opera, ballet); the 2,679-seat Concert Hall (symphony, jazz, dance, pop, and special events such as conventions); the 544-seat Drama Theatre (theater, musical theater,

Danish architect Jorn Utzon kept a Scandinavian touch to the project: The Opera House's "sails" are covered with one million Swedish ceramic tiles.

and contemporary dance); the smaller 398-seat Playhouse (plays, lectures, and seminars); and the newest addition, the 282-seat Studio (music and performing arts).

But the design of the building itself takes center stage, the star of the show.

Surely one of the 20th century's most masterful architectural statements, it is utterly original with its peaked white roofs shaped like sails or shells. Danish architect Jorn Utzon topped the field in an international competition to win the design job. Of the structure he predicted: "In the hot sun of the day it will be a beautiful, white shimmering thing—as alive to the eyes as architecture can make anything, set in the blue-

green waters of the harbor. And at night the floodlit shells will be equally vibrant—but in a soft, more majestic way."

Because the unique construction required engineers to invent new technology, the work took 14 years and came in a whopping 1,450 percent over budget, at 102 million Australian dollars. (The original projection was four years and seven

million Australian dollars.) The architect resigned part way through the project, after clashing with the engineers and government, and the design work was completed by local architects.

Today few people remember that controversy and only enjoy the beauty of the Opera House. In fact, this striking building put Sydney on the map. One Australian

With distinctive roofs shaped like sails—the highest rising 221 feet above the water—the Sydney Opera House stands on Bennelong Point in Sydney Harbor. Inside, visitors can find an opera theater, a concert hall, and a gourmet restaurant, all with stunning views of the water.

Member of Parliament observed that the Sydney Opera House was the greatest public-relations building since the Egyptian pyramids. He just might be correct.